proclamation

6 the Lessons of the Church Year

Susan K. Hedahl

EPIPHANY

PROCLAMATION 6 | SERIES A

FORTRESS PRESS | MINNEAPOLIS

PROCLAMATION 6
Interpreting the Lessons of the Church Year
Series A, Epiphany

Copyright © 1995 Augsburg Fortress. All rights reserved. Except for brief quotations in critical articles or reviews, no part of this book may be reproduced in any manner without prior written permission from the publisher. Write to: Augsburg Fortress, 426 S. Fifth St., Box 1209, Minneapolis, MN 55440.

Scripture quotations, unless otherwise noted, are from the New Revised Standard Version Bible, copyright © 1989 by the Division of Christian Education of the National Council of Churches in the U.S.A. and used by permission.

Library of Congress Cataloging-in-Publication Data

Proclamation 6. Series A : interpreting the lessons of the church year.
    p. cm.
    Contents: [1] Advent/Christmas / J. Christiaan Beker — [2] Epiphany / Susan K. Hedahl — [3] Lent / Peter J. Gomes — [4] Holy Week / Robin Scroggs.
    ISBN 0-8006-4207-4 (v. 1 : alk. paper). — ISBN 0-8006-4208-2 (v. 2 : alk. paper) — ISBN 0-8006-4209-0 (v. 3 : alk. paper) — ISBN 0-8006-4210-4 (v. 4: alk. paper)
    1. Bible—Homiletical use. 2. Bible—liturgical lessons, English.
BS534.5P74 1995
251—dc20   95-4622
                                                                          CIP

The paper used in this publication meets the minimum requirements of American National Standard for Information Sciences—Permanence of Paper for Printed Library Materials, ANSI Z329.48-1984. ∞™

Manufactured in U.S.A.   AF 1-4208

99   98   97   96   95   1   2   3   4   5   6   7   8   9   10

Contents

Introduction	5
The Epiphany of Our Lord	11
The Baptism of Our Lord *First Sunday after the Epiphany*	19
Second Sunday after the Epiphany	25
Third Sunday after the Epiphany	31
Fourth Sunday after the Epiphany	37
Fifth Sunday after the Epiphany	45
Sixth Sunday after the Epiphany	51
The Transfiguration of Our Lord *Last Sunday after the Epiphany*	57

Introduction

The primary question that the reader of this volume brings is, "How shall I preach this Epiphany season?" Since the form of a question generally presupposes its possible answers, the author reframes the proclamation query in this fashion: "Given the fragmentary nature of the historical record and witness, the poetic (even bizarre) imagery of some of the accounts, and the radical intersection of God and humanity on the boundaries of human experience and consciousness, how might our faith communities be assisted to re-envision these texts in their daily lives—anew?"

This means that the responses to the Epiphany texts are based on other concerns, of which exegesis and history are only two components. The basic perspective governing this work offers a *homiletical-rhetorical* vision that sets the proclaimer's question squarely within the faith community, past and current. Its primary dynamics operate in the array of textual and contemporary persuasive devices, including the mythopoetic images of many of the writings. As such this approach honors the fluidity of the community's language, witnesses to the depths of human religious experience and imagination, and incorporates the human responses of fear, awe, terror, and joy to God's epiphanic saving acts in Jesus Christ.

The rhetorical perspectives envisioned here push beyond the persuasive strategies of the spoken word. The texts themselves show what might be employed in our own proclamation—all sensory possibilities! Suggestions are offered in this regard that will enhance not only our proclamation, but also our people's experience and knowledge of God. What visions we have and words we hear are further enriched by the touch, fragrances, and tastes of the all-encompassing salvific graces of God among us.

This author—female, Christian, ordained, colleague, niece, aunt, daughter, seminary instructor—has found her own homiletical-rhetorical visions changed by this project. And the relationships named here, constitutive of her and her community, contain various reflections of gratitude for their contributions.

The words *Epiphany season* conjure up many images, chief of which are the biblical figures of the Magi, a star, and gifts. These images frequently translate into bathrobed children in Christmas plays with gold-painted stars hanging in the chancel. Above all, the texts point to one singular event and theme: the God who saves; salvation has been announced to everyone.

Epiphany is usually preached as an extension of Christmas and its symbols. Yet, this season also looks forward to the forthcoming Lenten calendar and another layer of symbols and themes. Before preaching, several major homiletical dynamics should be identified. They are recurrent imagery, themes and their chronological maturation, rhetorical enactments of the salvation story (which is both a textual and congregational issue), and the use of alternative readings.

First, regardless of the Sunday in this season, another core set of *images* is embedded in the texts, awaiting the proclaimer's investigations. These images occur frequently enough to provide a season-long framework for preaching.

Although Epiphany continues the season of the Christ Child, the texts demand a move beyond the well-known images toward a focus on others—light, water, the presence/absence of God, the cruciform shape of community, and images of barrenness and fruitfulness—that ask us to trade the religious sustenance of childhood for that of adulthood (see the epistle for the Sixth Sunday after the Epiphany).

These images, whether from the Old or the New Testament, may be used illustratively or thematically on a given Sunday or traced through the entire season. There is a humorous irony in these central images of the Epiphany lessons that forces a deeper consideration of the season itself because many Christians hear the texts in settings that are opposite from their own.

In a dark winter season, Epiphany proposes light, and not just a lightened corner but light that extends to the ends of the created order! As the waters of baptism splash resoundingly through several of the texts, congregants face the frozen snows of winter and many parishes face post-Christmas empty pews because of bad weather, illness, and holiday burnout. Where, then, is the cruciform shape of this people?

Epiphany works to energize when the inclination is hibernation! And yet, the images may be utilized to highlight the unique challenges of this season.

While light is in abeyance, what of the unexpected and beautiful mystical dance of the northern lights? What of the "snow angels" that adults and children trace in honor of things seen and unseen? What of the individual visits exchanged outside the gathered community that, in turn, reinforce its cruciform shape? What of the chinook winds that signal, in the middle of winter, a promise of coming fruition?

A second aspect of this season is featured in the *themes* or topics that the imagery bears. The season's texts cohere well and many of them continually reveal similar themes that may be preached as a series or

INTRODUCTION

separately. Most of the themes occur antithetically and are generally interrelated in each Sunday's set of lessons. Chief among these antitheses are despair and hope; enmity and reconciliation; wisdom and foolishness; imprisonment and release; sinfulness and accountability; obscurity and revelation; arrogance and humility; injustice and the accomplishment of justice.

Epiphany certainly presents the preacher with a decidedly trinitarian shape. The biblical passages highlight the God who creates a world out of nothing and calls people to life and to the light of salvation. This, in turn, points first, to the one who redeems—the one identified through the baptismal waters of the Jordan as God's Son, Jesus—and, secondly, to the work of the Spirit, in discussions of baptism, call, and community: how it is called, to whom it is accountable, the terrors it confronts, and the shape to which it is to conform.

A third component of the season relates to the *seasonal maturation of themes* initially presented during the feast day of the Epiphany. The ongoing readings from Isaiah, 1 Corinthians, and Matthew demonstrate the movement from introduction to development of the long-term challenges present to all people through the birth and ministry of Jesus.

The texts span the season not just sequentially but in a cumulative fashion. Jesus moves from the manger, to adult baptism, to the mountain with his disciples for instruction, and finally to his transfiguration. The prophets move through the landscapes of the despair of exile to the first signs of heartfelt redemption, even though the lands themselves might lie barren and devastation cover the territories. Paul invokes blessings on his Corinthian converts, despite the woefulness of their situation, and then progresses to challenge them honestly and bluntly about the meaning of true wisdom.

The preacher must also contend with an ongoing question that arises in all the texts from a variety of angles: What is the relationship of the Law (Torah) to Jesus' instructions? The Matthean formula signals similarities and differences: "You have heard it said . . . But I say to you. . . ."

The Hebrew Scriptures for Epiphany also contain this progression. The songs of Isaiah and the calls of the prophets urge the people to refuse to substitute cultic ritual for love of God and humanity. This is no mere abstract theological construct; rather, it becomes acutely urgent for contemporary listeners when such texts as the Matthean one on divorce are preached in the worshiping assembly.

Third, the *rhetorical shape and enactment* of texts is both a past and a current reality. It is imperative that the Epiphany proclaimer be aware of the wealth of the basic rhetorical shapes of the various texts. Prophetic oracles, theophanies, diatribes, covenantal ceremonies, epistolary forms, and liturgical poetry are not simply the shell casings of the "bullet," the unerring message of salvation. Rather, these chosen forms of speech demonstrate a godly and human sensitivity to the ears and condition of a given community now being addressed in its own unique historical context. Once the preacher knows these forms, he or she must next seek ways to shape rhetorically the text's message to the specific congregation. What persuasive strategies might most successfully honor the text's formation/content and the worshipers' presence?

Finally, perhaps the ultimate challenge for the Epiphany preacher as the twentieth century draws to a close is a way of taking into account the many possible *alternative readings* of a given text. It is urgent first of all that one's own "alternative reading" be clearly understood as it relates to others, stands in contrast to them, or confronts them with mixed feelings. By "alternative readings" I do not mean "variant readings" or possibilities related to the grammar and syntax of biblical texts, but rather the many theological perspectives that assist interpretation of Scripture.

The sources of such readings these days are numerous and sometimes conflict radically with one another: neighborhood interdenominational Bible studies; televised religious programs; the religious symbolism of MTV; theological works of all types; parish sermons; interpretations derived sheerly from the basis of personal faith experiences. The list is lengthy.

Three areas in particular can act as resources for the preacher during this season, primarily because the texts themselves bear the images, themes, and elements of what these resources represent. They are works from multicultural sources, from research in feminist biblical scholarship, and, finally, from the fine arts!

The central theme of Epiphany is the announcement of salvation to all people. If God has flung the net so wide, proclamation does well to mirror that action in its approaches. Other cultural-religious perceptions of God, and God's activities through Jesus, can enrich congregational life. One example of an alternative reading of texts—and therefore of preaching—comes from the "base communities" of South America. Records of the worship life show that textual imperatives, themes, and narratives are understood very differently from a North American context. The preacher can underscore the ethnic make-up of a congregation, its neighborhood, or its city, on the basis of the texts in such a way that evangelism *and* receiving the gifts of others are an appropriate Epiphany response to God's saving acts.

Another rich resource comes from the feminist biblical scholarship of the past twenty years. Scholars have presented new ways of reading and hearing texts; some have identified those texts that are damaging to women (and thus the entire community) and should be preached differently or not

INTRODUCTION

all. Other have pinpointed texts that have omitted women, although women have actually been present. Scholars have also discussed the dynamics of those texts that model right relationships in community between male and female and with God.

The Epiphany lessons for Year A require a new look in this regard. They contain a surprising cache of materials showing female images for primary religious symbols, women in leadership roles, maternal imagery used by male writers, and paradigms of new community that include all people. In keeping with one of the central themes of this season, justice, configurations of God's community may be thoughtfully brought to bear on the church's life.

Finally, the rich imagery and strange episodes recorded for Epiphany deserve proclamation that utilizes other art forms. The season's preaching should make a point of avoiding the strictly rationalistic, propositional types of sermon structures that do violence to what these texts propose in their mysterious, evocative presentations of the shifts in human consciousness in the presence of God! Different art forms may appeal to all the senses and serve to reinforce the homilist's words. Incense could be used on Epiphany, perhaps in a children's sermon, as a means of introduction to a liturgical act for traditions unaccustomed to its use. Paintings, glass pieces, textiles, and sculpted works can be placed on display for homiletical reference and corporate meditation, providing an interplay between verbal and visual forms of worship responses.*

As a visual and auditory art form, liturgical dance can also be used. The metaphoric possibilities of Epiphany, the Baptism of Our Lord, and the feast of the Transfiguration are appropriate times for this. One homiletical model from a seminary worship community may offer an example. The assigned text for the day was prefaced with readings from secondary theological sources in the tradition that reflected on the text. Excerpts were taken from the works of Augustine, Luther, Hildegard of Bingen, and Phyllis Trible. Following these readings, a dancer reenacted the text while it was simultaneously sung by a quartet to a psalm tone.

The Epiphany texts, the preacher, the people, and all their gifts and possibilities—these provide the matrix for what is most exciting about the season. Its theme of salvation for all people is actually an ongoing, self-reflexive meditation on one's own faith heritage. Epiphany, like the waters of baptism, gives us a moving mirror in which we see ourselves, and for a few brief moments, the shadow of the dove, the radiance of the Lord!

---

*Artist Geoffrey C. Thulin's watercolor diptych *Baptism into Light*, which hangs in the Gettysburg Lutheran Seminary chapel, provides an epiphanic motif that combines the shimmering effects of water and light—much like a swimmer close to breaking the surface into the air and sunshine.

As the texts indicate, God's salvation repeatedly and unexpectedly breaks through all boundaries to surprise and challenge with the announcement of salvation. Epiphany begins with the gift of the incarnation and, like a pebble thrown into a pool, ripples out with its implications and revelations for people in all times and places.

The Epiphany of Our Lord

Lectionary	First Lesson	Psalm	Second Lesson	Gospel
Episcopal	Isa. 60:1-6, 9	Psalm 72 or 72:1-2, 10-17	Eph. 3:1-12	Matt. 2:1-12
Roman Catholic	Isa. 60:1-6	Ps. 72:1-2, 7-8, 10-11, 12-13	Eph. 3:2-3a, 5-6	Matt. 2:1-12
Revised Common	Isa. 60:1-6	Ps. 72:1-7, 10-14	Eph. 3:2-12	Matt. 2:1-12
Lutheran	Isa. 60:1-6	Psalm 72	Eph. 3:2-12	Matt. 2:1-12

FIRST LESSON: ISAIAH 60:1-6, 9

Most of the first lessons for Epiphany in Year A come from the book of Isaiah. This selection is taken from the songs of Zion written by an individual or compiled by an unknown editor called "Third Isaiah."

This text is a song of dreams, hope, and certitude of salvation. It recapitulates the result of the hopes and activities reflected in other major Isianic texts throughout the Epiphany season, especially the Servant Songs of Second Isaiah.

In verse 1 the person addressed is a woman—Jerusalem or Zion. She is asked to rise from her place of darkness because her deliverance has come: "the glory of the Lord has risen upon you." The light she will shine with is not her own, but the reflected radiance of the Lord. The first three verses of this chapter reflect other Epiphany references to God's calling forth of the captive into light (Isa. 42:6-7).

The saved become, in turn, the abode of those others who also respond to the witness of Zion's own redemption. Redemption signifies a reversal in status since "nations" and "kings" will recognize and come to the restored Zion. Given women's lack of status and influence in ancient times, the figure of Zion as female makes the reversal particularly poignant and sharpens the contrast between the state of imprisonment and salvation.

Through the coming of the light, verses 2 and 3 describe how the one redeemed moves from obscurity to being the focus of attention, from unknown existence to high profile. In sum, the coming of salvation animates all of creation!

The hope of restoration marks these verses. It is the homecoming of everybody and everything. Verses 4 and 5 depict how both the animate and inanimate aspects of creation attest to the restoration of God's glory: the members of the clan return, the wealth of the land will pour forth, and the wealth of the soul will express itself (Isa. 49:18ab; 22de).

The Epiphany motifs of gifts and wealth, realized or impending, natural or humanly created, signal the gift of God's salvation and are lavished on the redeemed: "abundance of the sea"; "wealth of the nations"; "multitude of camels"; "gold and frankincense," "silver and gold."

Numerous contrasts in these verses show the impact of God's salvific acts: darkness and light, cast down and lifted up, disgrace and honor, isolation and community, poverty and wealth, the absence of God and God's presence, the distant and the proximate, the rejected and the esteemed, the mature and the youth.

The perimeters of the Lord's salvation extend beyond Israel to all nations, as indicated by their listing in verses 6 and 9 (see Genesis 10, which lists a "Table of Nations"). Not only the effects but also the scope of God's salvation can be both invitation and challenge to all who experience the limitlessness of God's activity.

SECOND LESSON: EPHESIANS 3:1-12

This reading is actually a digression from Paul's discussion of God's blessing of and call to the Ephesians. In these verses, Paul discusses the purpose and implication of his status as a prisoner and its relationship to the gospel. He has encountered significant problems through his claim and that the Gentiles share equally with the Jews in God's salvific acts.

In striking contrast to the release of the imprisoned in Isaiah, Paul shows that his very bondage also witnesses to God's salvation for all, Jew and Gentile. In verses 1-7 Paul casts his mission in the historical context of "former generations," "holy apostles and prophets," and the culmination of these events in the "revelation" to Paul of "the mystery of Christ."

Of particular importance is the word *mystery* in this text. While the word has a variety of New Testament meanings, here it refers to God's inclusion of the Gentiles in the plan of salvation. Paul reiterates God's purpose in several ways: the Gentiles should be esteemed as "fellow heirs," "members of the same body," "sharers in the promise" (v. 6).

Verse 8 may be read with the same understanding in that Christ's "unsearchable riches" (RSV) are not so much mysterious as limitless. They are accessible but never fully mined. Paul emphasizes the magnitude of God's gift in Christ through stressing his own insignificance in comparison to the message he brings. The "connector" or vital link that highlights God's salvation is grace.

It is noteworthy that the reality of "grace" is mentioned three times in this reading as the hinge upon which Paul's ministry operates. He has received a commission from God to do his ministry "for you" through God's grace (v. 2). He has been enabled to act as a servant because of "the gift of God's grace" (v. 7). And the focus of his ministry to the Gentiles has happened because of "this grace" (v. 8).

A charming, yet emphatic, new term is also introduced in verse 8, one probably of Paul's own devising. In his urgency to proclaim God's grace and great acts in contrast to the improbability of his own chosen servanthood, he describes himself as "the very least of all saints"! This delightful double entendre may well refer both to Paul's small physical stature and to what he perceives as the insignificance of his spiritual standing.

The "boundless riches" (v. 8) are not reserved for the sight of a few, but rather for "everyone to see." The statement repudiates both a gnostic and a nationalistic view of salvation. Additionally, God honors the church by expressing wisdom in the person of Jesus so that the "rulers and authorities in the heavenly places" might know "the plan of the mystery hidden for ages" (v. 10).

Verse 10 contains both a contextual note of importance and a rhetorical reversal. The wisdom of God will be made known in the church (*ekklesia*), in the community, an emphasis arising from the overall emphasis of Ephesians itself. The astonishing claim is made that it is the church that will instruct the *heavens* in God's wisdom! It is the church, in all its frailty, that will reveal God's wisdom "to the rulers and authorities in the heavenly places." Paul's statement is further confirmation that he is speaking not of private revelations of God's mysteries but of the community of the faithful, which in its own historical and visible mystery mirrors and contains God's wisdom.

The section concludes with Paul's sweeping assessment of the foundation of God's salvation in Jesus. It is situated "in accordance with the eternal purpose" (v. 11). Paul's assertion about "Christ Jesus our Lord" as the means by which God fulfills this purpose is important both in this context and as it relates to the same emphasis of the forthright messianic Christology of Matthew during this season. Similarly, Paul's post-resurrection retrospective view of Jesus also will be buttressed by the reading from John's Gospel for the Second Sunday after the Epiphany through the eloquent high Christology of the opening chapter.

Verse 12 notes that our "boldness" toward God emerges from our access to God through Jesus Christ. The word is significant in that the Greek primarily defines it as boldness of *speech*, not merely as an attitude or feeling of confidence. Thus the "boldness" of which Paul speaks is a public aspect of how the church will extend the news of Christ everywhere through its individual members.

Verse 12 is an appropriate conclusion to the digression. First, it reflects Paul's own history and his willingness to preach, despite his imprisonment and its possible consequences. Second, he advocates the same stance for his listeners, mindful of the possibilities of persecution that they, too, might face.

GOSPEL: MATTHEW 2:1-12

Matthew's Gospel is the only one to contain the story of the magi, popularly called "the three wise men" or "three kings." The legends, misreadings, and popular reenactments of this part of scripture have overshadowed the function of their appearance in Matthew's Gospel.

We know almost nothing of the magi—including their numbers, their ethnic background, their religious perspectives, the time of their journey, the reasons for it, and their societal status. They may have been part of a well-known class of professional astrologers, who, in Jesus' day, were sought out by a variety of people for their wisdom.

The extra-Christian and Jewish literature of the time shows that the anticipation of a new ruler was usually accompanied by a search in the zodiac for signs of his arrival. Most significant in the Judaic tradition with regard to messianic hopes is the prophetic oracle of Balaam (cf. Numbers 24:17), predicting that "a star shall come out of Jacob, and a scepter shall rise out of Israel. . . ."

Matthew's narrative is one more signal of the messianic Christology that dominates this gospel. The account draws on both the implicit historical connotations accorded the search for and sighting of a significant star and actual prophetic quotations to announce the birth of Jesus (Micah 5:2). Furthermore, Matthew emphasizes the specific topographical significance of Bethlehem in Judaic tradition by repeating the village's name four times in these verses (vv. 1, 5, 6, 8).

The overall climate in this episode, and the covert and cowering attitudes of most of the participants, contradict any sense of open expectation and joy that normally would accompany the birth of a king. Herod "was frightened, and all Jerusalem with him" (v. 3). The wise men, out of fear for their lives, do not return to Herod's presence.

Additionally, an air of secrecy prevails when Herod meets with the wise men in a private audience (v. 7). After consulting with both the temple personnel and the strangers, he issues an order in the truest form of hypocrisy (v. 8). The only expression of joy occurs when the sages rejoice before the infant Jesus and bestow their gifts (vv. 10 and 11).

Unlike the darkness that turns into light in the first lesson, the entire Matthean narrative takes place in darkness, both symbolic and actual. Herod meets in secret with the wise men, surreptitiously helpful but personally fearful of threats to his power. "All of Jerusalem" was frightened.

The wise men, in order to reach their destination, must have traveled at night in order to see the star at all. Both the landscape and the actions of the people highlight the star and the presence of the child. A warning from God to the wise men occurs in their sleeping hours—"in a dream."

THE EPIPHANY OF OUR LORD

In an eerie prefiguring of the later passion of Jesus, his days of infancy are already problematic as the wise men "left for their own country by another road." The passage stands in silhouette rather than in the sharp relief of the first lesson.

In keeping with Matthew's understanding of Jesus as the Son of God, the titles used to describe the infant in this narrative are important. There is nothing hidden about the child's identity in these verses: only human reaction to the birth is veiled and confused.

Jesus is called "the child who has been born king of the Jews" (v. 2); Herod asks "where the Messiah was to be born" (v. 4); through prophetic quotes Jesus is called "a ruler who is to shepherd my people Israel" (v. 6). Also, Matthew may have heightened his listeners' understanding of Jesus as God's Son (i.e., "child") by omitting any mention of Joseph.

HOMILETICAL REFLECTIONS

The primary homiletical challenge of this first Sunday in a brief liturgical season is to establish Epiphany as more than merely an extension of the memories of the Christmas season. One must attempt to move theologically and culturally beyond popular themes and images to some of the difficult and paradoxical problems raised by other poetic expressions of this season, such as in O. Henry's "The Gift of the Magi" and T. S. Eliot's *The Journey of the Magi.*

The texts of this entire season move very quickly within a Sunday to somber prophetic cries for salvation, to the conclusion of the birth narrative, to the turbulent era of the establishment of the church. Beginning with this first Sunday, the close links among the images, themes, and motifs of these lessons enable the preacher to open up the challenges and issues that direct the listeners toward the upcoming Lenten season. They can establish also a number of possible homiletical routes for successive Sundays in the season.

Epiphany proclamation offers, first of all, an evocative spectrum of images that the preacher may use either textually or thematically. All of the Epiphany Day lessons contain references to darkness and light, either explicitly or implicitly. The first two texts are set in the context of the darkness of imprisonment, while clearly the atmosphere of fear and constraint hangs over the Gospel lesson. These contrasting elements are related to the light of salvation, the brightness of dawn, the glory of the Lord, the radiance of the redeemed, the rising star, and the hiddenness of God's plan now revealed.

The use of light imagery in particular is significant in relationship to the current interest in fictional and biographical accounts of near-death or life-after-death experiences that feature light as an indication of God's presence. While the overly subjective interpretations given to such imagery can be questioned, the preacher nevertheless may find that parishioners resonate with the examples and that discussion of light is useful. In their totality, images of light and dark ultimately serve to reveal God in Jesus Christ to the nations.

Another image peculiar to all the texts is that of riches. Here the preacher can move beyond the wise men's gifts, possibly in ascending order, to note first the Isaian list of riches as indicators of God's salvific activities: riches of personal relationships, riches of the land and sea, and riches of God's presence in community.

Paul's relationship with God speaks of "the gift of God's grace," those who are "heirs," "the news of the boundless riches of Christ," and "the wisdom of God in its rich variety." Finally, although the Gospel text begins with Herod's hypocritical desire to "pay him homage" and with the gifts of the magi, it culminates in the magi's response to God's salvation at the sight of the child—"they were overwhelmed with joy."

Riches, as an Epiphany theme, however, is problematic since the riches may just as easily turn the recipient against God as signify an expression of God's goodness. As the season progresses, the texts teach that lavish gifts are no substitute for true worship; poverty of spirit is desirable, and the absence of riches in the Pauline passages indicates the abundance of Christ's "unsearchable riches." The preacher may wish to argue a "have and have-not" thematic sermon in this regard.

The overarching heart of Epiphany proclamation is the gift of God's salvation to all humanity, in all times and places. Thus, two possible approaches to the day's texts may be particularly useful: First, in a general way, the preacher can develop and establish the reality of God's revelation throughout the season by addressing that initially through this Sunday's text. She or he might plan the entire sermon series with the idea of both God's immediate gift in Jesus and the gradual revelation of his person and purposes in the hearts and communities of the faithful through time.

Such an approach (actually an implicit preaching program for the entire Epiphany season) may be useful in terms of evangelism. Certainly, committed seekers of all sorts may yet be unfamiliar with who is revealed in Jesus Christ and what that implies for their lives.

Second, and more specifically, this day's texts also need realistically to highlight and heighten the problematic context of this gift. This gift is one not necessarily readily acknowledged or accepted—or perhaps even known. Its arrival may even be actively rejected, feared, and temporarily defeated, a fact to which both the second lesson and Gospel clearly attest. It is a gift that comes in the midst of human struggles and fears and is continually

THE EPIPHANY OF OUR LORD

susceptible to the compelling and destructive forces of ethnicity, power, social status, and control. It is a gift that is fragile and vulnerable to acceptance, rejection, or attempted destruction. Everything rests on the beginnings of, simply, a new baby. The realities that these texts address are clearly no different in some forms earlier than those today.

Quite conceivably listeners may, in their personal and corporate lives, experience the delay or deformation of God's gift as it attempts to break through humanity's barriers, ones erected by the self as well! The preacher's task is to emphasize clearly the good news of the Epiphany Day texts, mindful of their significance in a contemporary context.

The Baptism of Our Lord
First Sunday after the Epiphany

Lectionary	First Lesson	Psalm	Second Lesson	Gospel
Episcopal	Isa. 42:1-9	Ps. 89:1-29 or 89:20-29	Acts 10:34-38	Matt 3:13-17
Roman Catholic	Isa. 42:1-4, 6-7	Ps. 29:1-4, 9-10	Acts 10:34-38	Matt. 3:13-17
Revised Common	Isa. 42:1-9	Psalm 29	Acts 10:34-43	Matt. 3:13-17
Lutheran	Isa. 42:1-7	Ps. 45:7-9	Acts 10:34-38	Matt. 3:13-17

FIRST LESSON: ISAIAH 42:1-7

This text has been identified as the first of four "Servant Songs" in the portion of Isaiah named Deutero-Isaiah (cf. 49:1-6; 50:4-9; 52:13—53:12). Authorship of these works is unknown, as is the specific identity of the servant.

Who is this servant? It could be the nation of Israel, the author of the song, an unknown prophet. Some think it might be a reference to Cyrus of Persia, considered by some to have been the instrument of God's instruction and discipline for the people of Israel in the midst of the death and chaos he caused.

Just as this servant is spoken "about" rather than "to," so the servant's call and mission are described as activities carried out indirectly and quietly. This becomes particularly important when one considers that the servant's *mission*, rather his identity, that is of essential interest. Whether the identity of the servant is understood as singular or ambiguously plural, his mission is initially introduced in verses 1-4 through repetition of a specific cluster of words.

The first four verses repeat the word *justice* three times (vv. 1, 3, 4). In order to understand what justice means, note that the word is linked in verse four with the word *teaching*. This broadens the word *justice* to include not only law in the judicial sense but also wisdom, knowledge that should constitute a way of life for individuals and nations. In other words, one achieves justice through the path of wisdom, resulting in God's revelation to all the nations.

The opening verse sounds like an introduction to a ruler's court. The speaker, the LORD, presents the Servant as pleasing, graced by the Spirit and with a mission whose success is assured. The introduction is not just "pro forma," for the ruler obviously holds the servant in high esteem, since he is called "my chosen, in whom my soul delights" (v. 1).

Significant in these first four verses is the servant's *modus operandi*. The mission's accomplishment will occur in neither grandiose nor possibly even discernible ways. The verses state this in a negative fashion; that is, what the servant will not do. This will not be business as usual. "He will not cry or lift up his voice" (v. 2); nor break a bruised reed or quench a dimly burning wick (v. 3). "He will not grow faint or be crushed" (v. 4). All of these possibilities may be fairly expected for so daunting a task. Things could get lost in the rush. Considering the scope and difficulty of the servant's work and responsibilities, it is paradoxical that he will accomplish justice in such a quiet, sensitive way.

The striking use of the images of a dimly burning wick and a bruised reed emphasize both the frailty of the condition and hopes of those who await salvation. Everything hangs in the balance. Even an act of thoughtlessness—let alone outright malice—can destroy those who are without light or hope. Such imagery certainly indicates the servant's attention to the less obvious, but equally important, aspects of the lives of God's people.

The reasoning of these verses inspires confidence in the servant who will eventually bring forth the fruits of justice (vv. 1, 3); who will exhibit a patient and fruitful restraint (v. 2), and see the conclusion of the mission (v. 4). The outcome of the servant's mission is not described merely in probable terms but in terms expressing confidence in future success.

Verse 5 forms a linking verse to the next two. It emphasizes the attributes and acts of the one who calls the servant. The servant is not greater than the LORD. This LORD is named as the one who engenders all life, the one who hosts the servant's forthcoming mission.

Verses 5-7 may be considered as a response and amplification of the statements of the first four verses. Verse 6 focuses on the breathtaking scope of the Servant's mission; it is to "all nations." Further, the goal of the LORD's covenant is to illuminate the nations.

Just as prisoners sit both in bondage and without light as a result (v. 7), so shall the nations receive enlightenment and release. Like last week's Isaiah text, the same setting of movement from darkness to light through God's agency gives release and salvation. Again, whether that mission is accomplished through the individual servant, the nation, or even an alien ruler, Cyrus of Persia, is not the main focus of these verses; rather, it is the content and direction of the mission that intends the salvation of all.

SECOND LESSON: ACTS 10:34-38

These four verses form the beginning of one of Peter's mission speeches, or sermons, to the centurion Cornelius and his household. The men's meeting together is cast in the greater context of God's appearance to both of them previously: each man has been brought into the other's company by a vision. The effect of these visions dissolves the usual boundaries of

THE BAPTISM OF OUR LORD

race and society between the two and Peter is asked to speak the Lord's commands to Cornelius and his people.

Verses 34-35 begin with a statement about the source of salvation: the God who shows no partiality or, literally, "accepts no one's face." This word reflects a unique blend of judgment and grace. It comes from the God whose peculiar lack of discrimination has, in fact, brought Peter and Cornelius into one another's company as such an example: two men who would otherwise be separated by the social and ethnic standards and values of their day.

In verse 36 Jesus is named in relationship to the accomplishment of God's activities: "He is Lord of all." As in other lessons, God's salvific intentions are related to "every nation" (v. 35). Verse 37 announces Christ's lordship within the context of its prefiguring in John's baptismal ministry.

Verse 38 refers to God's anointed, Jesus, and the good that Jesus does comes from God's presence in him. "Doing good" and "healing" emerge because of Jesus' anointing. Jesus' actions flesh out the Isaian metaphor of an imprisoned people released from their confinement.

The meaning of anointing in verse 38 corresponds to its mention in Isaiah 61:1-2. Additionally, there are echoes of Luke's Gospel when anointing follows Jesus' baptism and his temptation in the wilderness, respectively (cf. 3:22 and 4:14). Jesus' first public address to people (Luke 4:18-19) is contingent on God's anointing. In these New Testament references the anointing is done in connection with God's presence and purpose—salvation is extended to all the nations. Mention is also made in verse 38 of two gifts bestowed with the anointing: a paired reality found repeatedly in other New Testament texts—"Holy Spirit and power." (See the Fifth Sunday after the Epiphany).

GOSPEL: MATTHEW 3:13-17

An air of bewilderment prefaces the act of Jesus' baptism by John. Why is *Jesus* asking to be baptized? The tradition provides many clues and possible answers that reflect the multifaceted radiance of the act of baptism itself in the lives of the faithful!

Accounts of Jesus' baptism are recorded in all four Gospels, with some variations. Only Matthew's Gospel contains John's initial refusal (vv. 14-15) and Jesus' response about the necessity of the baptism.

Typical of Matthean emphasis is his use of the word *righteousness* (v. 15). Jesus' rejoinder to John is that his baptism constitutes a *fulfillment* of righteousness. Matthew's Gospel reflects an understanding of Jesus both as *fulfillment* (e.g., his use of Isaiah) of the prophecies and also as *identification*; that is, Jesus acts as the representative of the new humanity wrought through salvation.

Of interest then and now, the verses report a heavenly acclamation following the baptism. The "voice from heaven" is a common term found in rabbinic literature and is delightfully translated as "daughter of a voice" (Hebrew: *bath-kol*). That is to say, the voice is an echo, a mediated communication of the living God. The use of the demonstrative "this" shows that in Matthew's account, a crowd witnessed to the voice.

Jesus is named both "Beloved" and "Son" (the terms have differing meanings). While "Son" is self-explanatory (see also Ps. 2:7), "Beloved" connotes a variety of sources. It is used in this Sunday's Isaiah text, Isaac is called this in Genesis 22:2. Most importantly for the season, the voice will repeat the same imperative in the text for the Feast of the Transfiguration (see Matthew 17). The combined terms of "Beloved" and "Son" paradoxically connote the possibilities of both an identification of Jesus with a Davidic-descended Messiah as well as the self-identified servant of humanity.

What of the sign of the dove in these verses? This is a rabbinic symbol for the people of Israel and a sign used extensively for the bride in the Song of Songs. Whether the dove is considered as a simile, "like the Spirit," or metaphorically as the enspirited dove, this sign is rich in historical meaning for those who experienced its presence.

The question remains, Why was Jesus baptized? The text provides some possible answers, particularly when read in conjunction with other Gospel accounts. The baptism could have signified a prefiguring of the death Jesus would suffer. He was certainly fulfilling the divine mandate to enter into this aspect of his ministry. Or his acquiesence to the action can be understood as a willing assumption of his mission and acknowledgment of his identity publicly as the one of God's own choosing. Whatever the choices made in this regard, Jesus' baptism is linked at many levels with those of the faithful in every time and place.

HOMILETICAL REFLECTIONS

In many congregations following a baptism the pastor will customarily scoop up the child in her arms and walk through the congregation with him. Parishioners, both adults and children, are introduced closeup to the newest member of the tribe, by name.

If one were to ask the question, "What's in a name?" according to today's texts—everything! Naming denotes identity, mission, goal, and relationships for both Jesus and his disciples.

THE BAPTISM OF OUR LORD

This particular feast day offers wonderful homiletical possibilities for emphasizing the role and purposes of baptism, and the content of the baptismal vows that all are called to live out. The similarities *and* the differences between our baptisms and Jesus' own can also be incorporated into the sermon.

Preachers may wish to identify particular baptismal themes as they relate specifically to the Epiphany season; for instance, the call of God, doing justice, mission to all the nations. Because of the plethora of themes and realities posed by baptism, the rite may be perceived in very different ways depending on its seasonal context.

The theme of *introductions* is featured predominantly in all the day's lessons. They serve the function of answering the question, "Who is this anyway?" These introductions are more than those espoused by "Miss Manners." Not only honor and politeness are at stake, but basic questions of identity and purpose. The new order of life in Christ, foretold and inaugurated in Jesus and spoken to the nations, underscores the importance of introductions. Going into a strange land unannounced may have its dangers!

Isaiah's opening words portray a member of royalty introducing a beloved servant to the court. Jesus' emergence from the Jordan is accompanied with an introduction from God, and Peter introduces Cornelius and his household to the person and mission of Jesus Christ: "I present to you. . . ."

While introductions may say "This is who this is," they also serve the dual function of showing support and the witness of others to the individual's acts and claims. This is reflected in this day's texts in that Jesus is spoken "about" but does not speak directly on his own behalf.

The epistle text, in particular, offers possibilities for a rhetorical reshaping that can emphasize this. The current lectionary listing includes only the beginning of Peter's sermon. In order to preach the extent of Peter's intentions with Cornelius and his household, the homilist may explore the general features of Petrine missionary sermon structure as found in Acts and offer a sermon in that vein, with appropriate Epiphany emphases.

The context of Peter's sermon is a direct example of the individual instances of "all nations" having dealings with one another through their commonality of faith. Lest the visions and the meeting at Cornelius' house seem merely part of the historical record, this account may be held alongside current instances of worldwide massive slaughter resulting from obsessive nationalism. The bravery and faithfulness and willingness of both men to meet and talk is more crucial than might be thought at first reading.

Certainly, the achievement of justice and peace in the name of the Christ who preaches it continues to haunt the world's battlegrounds.

The themes of this Epiphany time present a microcosm of the processes and role of time in relationship to God's saving acts. They show that God's people live between the accomplished and the yet-to-come. To live on only one side of the equation, however, is to succumb either to despair or complacency.

The current evidence is obvious: justice has not yet been accomplished. Despite the high esteem in which the unnamed servant is held, the tasks ahead will prove daunting. Bruised reeds are still being regularly trod underfoot and dimly burning wicks are flaming out everywhere. The One who emerges from the waters of baptism has everything yet ahead of him, as do those who are baptized into his name.

The texts as a group offer introductions, mission, and baptism as signs of eschatological tension and high drama. They also offer invitation to involvement.

Peter's sermon reveals a reflection of a people who are definitely a work-in-progress, with much to learn on all sides. In these eight Sundays of Epiphany, the unaccomplished is to be stressed as much as the foreordained. After "seeing the light," shaking off the waters of baptism and looking ahead, the people of God are being called to a deepening of their lives and knowledge.

Just as the lessons understand history and God's actions as indirect and subtle, so they reflect the very person of the Messiah who works in the same way. As the Isaian texts show, he is one who moves gracefully, unexpectedly in a hidden manner, with the seismographs of eternity poised for a final, tumultuous revelation.

Second Sunday after the Epiphany

Lectionary	First Lesson	Psalm	Second Lesson	Gospel
Episcopal	Isa. 49:1-7	Ps. 40:1-10	I Cor. 1:1-9	John 1:29-41
Roman Catholic	Isa. 49:3, 5-6	Ps. 40:2, 4, 7-10	I Cor. 1:1-3	John 1:29-34
Revised Common	Isa. 49:1-7	Ps. 40:1-11	I Cor. 1:1-9	John 1:29-42
Lutheran	Isa. 49:1-6	Ps. 40:1-12	I Cor. 1:1-9	John 1:29-41

FIRST LESSON: ISAIAH 49:1-6

These verses contain the second of the so-called Servant Songs of Second Isaiah. Here the speaker is not the Lord but the servant, and the mood shifts several times. The structure of these verses, each triadic in form, reflects the experience of those called by God.

The first four verses of this chapter parallel those of Isaiah 42:1-4. Verses 1-4 speak of the servant's election, call (not the same as election), and equipping for ministry. Verse 4 depicts the all too familiar reaction of despondency on the part of the servant: ministry often seems to have no results, and even the exertion of all of one's energy may seem fruitless. Yet, the servant reasserts confidence both in God as the source of the call and the reward that will follow.

Finally, verses 5 and 6 demonstrate the mighty acts of God in the servant's life through the rhetorical technique of "gradatio." Not only has the servant been fitted for ministry, but an even greater set of tasks will be added on to the ones already entrusted to him. This addition is truly a sign of God's love and favor!

The opening strophe, or section, of these verses is rich in allusion. Confessional in nature, this servant's affirmation of the call of God resembles other Old Testament records of God's call. Verse 1b is similar in nature to Jeremiah's call (cf. Jeremiah 1:5).

Examples of God's claim, as prior to all others, can be found in Psalm 22:10-11 and Psalm 139:13-16, and these demonstrate that this call is preordained and preexistent in the life of the Servant.

The Hebrew traditions associated with the power of the word far exceed our contemporary understandings of the power of speech, possibly because we live in a more visual than verbal culture. In this section, the medium for revelation and the call of God to the servant is the spoken word of God rather than a visual experience; "The Lord called me before I was born" (v. 1). In turn, this word that creates or destroys, curses or blesses, will fill the prophet who will, in turn, use speech on behalf of God's people.

Two martial images—the sharp sword and the polished arrow—highlight the servant's prophetic abilities in verse 2 (cf. Jer. 23:29; Heb. 4:12; Eph. 6:17; Rev. 1:16; Rev. 19:15 for references to Isa. 49:2). The power of the prophet's speech will destroy the enemies of Israel and protect the faithful from harm.

Additionally, the hiddenness of God's salvific plans is indicated by the phrase "shadow of his hand." Revelation must await its time, and, like the shade tree in the desert, God will keep sheltered that whose time is yet to come. (For a Pauline parallel, see 1 Corinthians 4:1-5).

Verse 3 is sometimes considered problematic due to the inclusion of the word *Israel*, possibly by a later editor. Whatever the referent of "servant," however, whether individual or corporate in nature, God's call is still the primary focus of this passage.

The term *suffering servant* seems to stem from the prophet's conflicts as indicated in verse 4. His sufferings, while distinct, are not unique to the reception of prophetic words in the life of Israel (cf. Isa. 6: 9-11; Mark 4:12, Matt. 11:15-17).

Verse 5 provides the servant's prologue to the Lord's response. The Lord's response to the servant comes in the form of added work and blessing. The servant learns that the mission to Israel is to extend into all nations. This parallels the same assertion found in the first Servant Song in Isaiah 42:6. In sum, the dialogical pattern of these verses reveals a blossoming and widening of mission to include all nations.

SECOND LESSON: I CORINTHIANS 1:1-9

The second lesson, like the first, features the matter of God's call, a call now shown specifically to emerge through Jesus Christ. Unlike the contents of the first lesson, however, this discussion of God's call is centered in a specific community of believers.

Evidence of this may be derived from the name of Sosthenes mentioned in verse 1, who was a Jewish convert. Couched in epistolary form, the identity of the servant, the "apostle," is also known—Paul.

The verses of this lesson are typical in many ways of the greetings and thematic forms of letters written in the early Christian era. Names and themes to be developed later in the letter are all expressed at an early point.

Paul begins by speaking to the church or *ekklesia* in Corinth. The term could refer to any profane or sacred gathering and thus is not specifically ecclesiastical in our contemporary sense. Paul stresses that the common ground of the unity of the group is its sanctification in Christ Jesus. The assembly is not of itself holy except inasmuch as its sanctity is a gift of God in Jesus Christ.

SECOND SUNDAY AFTER THE EIPIHANY

In his wish to them for grace and peace (v. 3), Paul combines both Greek and Hebrew realities. "Grace" refers to the giftedness of God's presence and "peace" reflects the salvific quality of life lived in a state of grace.

The term *Lord*, applied to Jesus, is particularly significant in that it was also used of secular authorities of that day. To affirm Jesus as Lord was making both a faith assertion and a daring social statement.

After concluding the preliminaries, Paul begins in verses 4-9 with a form of thanksgiving for the lives and activities of the people of Corinth. In general, his statements certainly reflect God's grace and peace, given the problems that have elicited the letter.

That Paul is able to thank God for his converts at Corinth (v. 4) indicates his belief in a God who redeems. The problems in the Corinthian community almost, but not quite, defy Paul's intervention and solutions. Yet, in the face of these problems, Paul gives thanks.

Paul begins positively, by pointing out what the conflicted community already possesses on which to build. In knowledge as well as in speech, God has given them everything! Later, Paul will sharply criticize the Corinthians' abuse of the gifts of knowledge (see 1:18—2:5; 8:1-3) and speech (cf. chaps. 12-14). This criticism stands in ironic contrast with the earlier tone of thanksgiving. Paul's ordering of praise and blame suggests that God may forgive and renew what has become distorted and abused.

Paul wants the Corinthians to know the goal and purpose of their God-derived gifts, as he reminds them in verses 5 and 6, and that these enhance their wait for Jesus' return. In order to reiterate the importance of this reality, verse 7 repeats verse 5, only in negative form.

The eschatological view appears again in verse 8 as Paul introduces a theme that was central for the early church, the Day of our Lord Jesus Christ. Like the earlier repetition, this is a variation of verse 7. (See also Old Testament references to this idea in Amos 5:18 and later in Phil. 1:6, 10 and 1 Thess. 3:13, 5:23).

It is both ironic and tender-hearted of Paul to term the Corinthians "blameless" in his hopes for them on the final day. Indeed, he says this knowing how culpable they are in their life as a church and how that demands an open and honest confrontation on his part.

The opening thanksgiving ends with the rationale for his former statements. God is the one who calls. God is the one who is faithful to the terms of the call. God will accomplish what God intends. This may be seen from the partial revelation already given: Jesus Christ, the risen Lord, will be the final revelation to the Corinthians of what they now only experience in part.

GOSPEL: JOHN 1:29-41

Following the lofty and revelatory beauty of this chapter's opening prologue, John focuses on the historical events surrounding the relationship between John the Baptist and Jesus.

On the second day of the evangelist's explanation of events, Jesus appears and the Baptist hails him as the Lamb of God (v. 29). John's acclamation could reflect any of several strands of the Hebrew faith tradition: for example, the paschal lamb (cf. John 19:36; Exod. 12:46; Num. 9:12), the rich and vivid apocalyptic references in the rabbinic and testamental literature to the lamb and possibly the suffering servant of Isaiah 53 (vv. 7, 10, 12). The book of Revelation contains twenty-eight references to the exalted Christ as the Lamb.

John's version of Jesus' baptism in verses 29-34 differs significantly from that of the Synoptics. John presents a specific view of Jesus: he was preexistent (v. 30) and his revelation to Israel is covered in secrecy, not even obvious to John himself (vv. 31, 33). The emphasis in these verses falls not on the event of Jesus' baptism so much as on John's response to it and his presentation of Jesus. This is underscored by the text's silence on John's actual baptism of Jesus!

The evangelist then turns to what is understood as the third day of events, verses 35-42. This section repeats John's acclamation of Jesus as the Lamb of God (v. 36).

Two disciples follow Jesus. In contrast to the Synoptic accounts, he does not call them to follow! In fact, he questions them about their presence (v. 38), and they in turn persist and want to know where he is staying. Only Andrew is identified as one of the two disciples. His response to Jesus is significant, since he identifies Jesus as the Messiah.

Some sources speculate that the omission, accidental or purposeful, of the other disciple's name introduces the figure called the "beloved disciple."

The *titles* used in this section derive from a number of sources and are important for the proclaimer's Epiphany task of identifying Jesus as God's Son and as Messiah. The appellation "Lamb of God" is added to "rabbi" (v. 38), a term commonly applied to those who taught. John uses the term frequently in the first part of his Gospel (called the Book of Signs), but then changes to "Lord" (*kyrios*) in the latter half (Book of Glory). "Messiah" or "anointed one" is used here as a translation from the Aramaic and occurs in the New Testament only here and in John 4:25. The titles John and his disciples use for Jesus represent the different layers of understanding, tradition, and insight into the person and actions of Jesus.

HOMILETICAL REFLECTIONS

All the lessons for this Sunday contain the reality, implicitly or explicitly, of "mission." Taken as a group, the three texts give concrete form to the call of God as it manifests itself to the individual and communities.

Isaiah's words present the realistic—and dialogic—nature of God's call and human response, which may legitimately include feelings of futility and despair. Can God really do this—through me? The introduction to Paul's letter sketches out the Corinthians' problems as well as God's gifts and presence among them.

Jesus' own baptism, understood as the sealing of his mission, also highlights other elements of God's call, particularly the theme of hiddenness. Isaiah places the servant in the position of waiting for God's own good time of enacting salvation. Paul's letter demonstrates that hiddenness is also experienced in waiting for God (v. 7).

Both John and his disciples experience the workings of discernment as they attempt to see who and what Jesus is, what is hidden in this rabbi's nature. The disciples' curiosity and the way they follow Jesus give evidence of this.

Undoubtedly, God's call may began quietly, even obscurely among ordinary people. It could very well also continue to work itself out in that context! The contours of the call may be unclear and allegiance to it a process of ongoing definition, which demands both patience and faith.

Both the Gospel and the epistle texts inevitably focus on baptism. Yet, this feast day celebrates not the baptism of the faithful but *Jesus'* baptism, and this means preaching that action with different emphases. What liturgical and homiletical riches are available? The Gospel text gives the clue. The focus is not on the baptism itself but on the various dialogues that occur around it and following it. John and the disciples express their questions, curiosity, and faith affirmations about the meaning of Jesus' baptism, personhood, and nature.

Preachers may wish to begin with or focus an entire sermon on the significance of baptism for Jesus as the inauguration of his ministry. Or they can choose to speak of the call to discipleship that emerges from baptism, vocation, and their place within the community of believers. The last issue can be understood also in relationship to the problems Paul addresses in the Corinthian community.

Since the texts contain many important "signal" words in the Christian tradition the textual, historical, or liturgical meanings of any of them could be explored: Lamb of God, the Anointed One, grace and peace, the Day of Our Lord Jesus Christ, Messiah. The words are rich with eschatological and sacramental meanings.

The lessons also hold up an existential mirror to the problems emerging from our baptismal vocation and the ways in which they unfold in our lives. Living out the call is not necessarily a smooth process! The very fact that people may understand their baptismal vows differently frequently gives rise to unrest within communities of the faithful, some of whom may become alarmed at the roads taken by others because of their own understanding of how to be faithful to God. Congregational "splits," disputes, and problems can be one possible manifestation of this fact.

Since these are always realities in some corners of the communion of saints, the texts can be preached as a pastoral response to the fact that our calls differ and to the issues thereby raised. Paul's own response to the Corinthians is a primary example of his mixed feelings about these converts to whom God had given "everything"! And yet, they were still embattled over the meanings of their baptisms.

Individually, each text provides several options. Isaiah's text can be preached in terms of the glory and joy of the previous Sunday's Isaian passage. There the call is a glorious experience. This Sunday's words show the need for patience and the healing of despair and frustration on the part of the servant. It also demonstrates God's faithfulness to the servant and the added gifts of affirmation in ever increasing ministry possibilities. While the first fervor of call often gives way to depression or disinterest, the servant finds that eventually God brings renewal of vision and energy.

The Corinthian lesson may be read in the form of a possible magna carta for a congregation's new year (both liturgical and chronological). Despite the problems, Paul expresses his love for his people and for the heart of their community, hope, and expectations—Jesus Christ. This text is clear evidence that expectations of untroubled community life, lived under the call of God, are unrealistic. Faithfulness to baptismal calling, however, is the basis for this life.

Finally, the Gospel text offers many opportunities to emphasize elements that differ from the Synoptics in this account of Jesus' baptism: John's central role as the herald of Jesus' ministry; disciples who follow out of curiosity rather than being called, the reiteration of the rich acclamation "Lamb of God!" This latter phrase may be tied homiletically to the baptismal and the eucharistic life of the congregation. Since the context for the passage from John is set by the prologue with its high Christology, the role of God's Son as Messiah may bear mention.

Whatever the identity of the "beloved disciple," it is a wonderful device to enhance the ownership, importance, and reality of God's call for each Christian. Since the texts describe only the call of male disciples, an historical reality with contemporary problems, the figure of the beloved disciple is a helpfully inclusive one. As with the bowed heads of the disciples in Salvador Dalí's painting *The Last Supper*, in most cases it is difficult to tell whether men or women or both are seated with Jesus at the table.

Third Sunday after the Epiphany

Lectionary	First Lesson	Psalm	Second Lesson	Gospel
Episcopal	Amos 3:1-8	Ps. 139:1-17 or 139:1-11	I Cor. 1:10-17	Matt. 4:12-23
Roman Catholic	Isa. 8:23—9:3	Ps. 27:1, 4, 13-14	I Cor. 1:10-13, 17	Matt. 4:12-23 or 4:12-17
Revised Common	Isa. 9:1-4	Ps. 27:1, 4-9	I Cor. 1:10-18	Matt. 4:12-23
Lutheran	Isa. 9:1b-4 or Amos 3:1-8	Ps. 27:1-9	I Cor. 1:10-17	Matt. 4:12-23

FIRST LESSON: ISAIAH 9:1-4

These verses form the first part of a messianic oracle that comes from First Isaiah. (In its original context, it might have been written to celebrate the accession of a Judean king). One who preaches an Epiphany sermon on this text may wish to include the entire rhetorical unit, which ends with verse 7, since the lection cuts it off after verse 4. This passage is also significant for year A in that part of it is quoted in the day's Gospel (Matt. 4:15-16) and the historical rationale for the inauguration of Jesus' Galilean ministry is thereby established.

It is unknown whether the king referred to as "he" and "you" is actual or ideal, past or to come. Freedom in these verses refers to both freedom from the oppressor and freedom to live on the land. The lands referred to in verse 1 were ruled by Assyria, even the coastal areas (cf. 2 Kings 15:29).

Just as in other key Isaiah passages, including Isaiah 49:6, the theme of a new light comes into play in v. 2. The freedom of release is expressed in verse 3 through images of the harvest and a triumphant militia dividing the spoils of war. In both cases, the people increase or resupply what they lack.

Verse 4 continues the military imagery: The enemy of the people has been routed just as it has been through Gideon's complete victory over the invading Midianites (cf. Judges 6–8, especially 7:15-25). Verse 4 also describes the peoples' dehumanizing oppression by the enemy in terms of the way beasts of burden are treated: "the yoke of their burden," "the bar across their shoulder."

The "rod of the oppressor" was not simply captivity hyperbole (see Exod. 21:20). The employment of corporal punishment (the "yoke") in order to subdue the people, and the tragic consequences of this action, also figure in the life of one of the early kings (cf. 1 Kings 12:1-15).

FIRST LESSON: AMOS 3:1-8

The beginning of chapter three marks the first of what scholars understand to be the three major divisions of Amos' material; this section continues through the end of chapter 6. Amos confronts Israel for its sin in blunt terms.

Amos describes the intense relationship between God and Israel. So bonded are the two that Lord is compelled to punish the people for their sins. God's reasons and purposes are emphasized through a series of questions in verses 3-6.

Verse 6 links God's actions to a people's punishment for the sins (cf. Isa. 45:7). The prophets warned the people that actions have consequences. Significantly, the prophets are identified as "servants" in verse 7. Other identifications of the prophet as God's servant may be found in Genesis 18:17-19; Exod. 4:15-16; Jeremiah 7:25; Daniel 9:10; Luke 1:70; and in the writings of Paul. This prophet-as-servant motif figures through many of the Epiphany season texts.

SECOND LESSON: I CORINTHIANS 1:10-17

This text continues Paul's thinking from last Sunday. The issues referred to then only obliquely are now identified clearly: The church at Corinth was involved in theological disputes that were affecting community life as a whole. The paraenetic emphasis of the address is immediately apparent through Paul's use of the phrase, "I appeal to you. . . ."

Paul has been prompted to write his letter because of reports he has received from "Chloe's people," either written or firsthand accounts of the problems (v. 11). While verse 12 lists four persons who might represent four divisions of thinking, Paul proceeds to challenge their affiliations over the issue at hand by posing three questions in verse 13. The answer to each of them is obviously "No!"

The "quarrels" referred to in verse 11 apparently have to do with the efficacy of baptism in relation to the person doing the baptizing. Paul rejects the notion that the identity of the baptizer has any significance: the relationship between baptized and baptizer is not the point of baptism!

Significant also in verse 13 is Paul's linkage of baptism with Christ's crucifixion (Romans 6:3ff.). Matthew does not make this connection although it does appear in John's Gospel, particularly with John's threefold reference to the "Lamb of God."

In verses 14-16 Paul expresses saracastic relief that he is exempt from the Corinthians' disputes since he only baptized Crispus, Gaius, and the household of Stephanas. (For accounts of other household baptisms, see Acts 11:14-15; 16:15, 32, 34; and 18:8). His decision to exempt himself

THIRD SUNDAY AFTER THE EPIPHANY

from the issue of baptism does not decrease its importance, however, as verse 17 shows. This verse, through the use of three negatives, defines more clearly what Paul understands his mission to be: "Christ did not send me to baptize"; he came "not with eloquent wisdom," in order that the cross "might not be emptied of its power." Paul's mission is not to baptize, but "to proclaim the gospel."

Since this text continues into future Sundays, it is important to note that the words *wisdom* and *power* in the final verse will serve as the keys to Paul's continuing dialogue with the Corinthians.

GOSPEL: MATTHEW 4:12-23

This passage follows the account of Jesus' temptation in the wilderness and marks the inauguration of his public ministry in Galilee. Like the epistle text, this section is linked to troubling issues related to baptism—in this case John's arrest, which forces Jesus to change geographical locale.

Verses 13-16 show that Jesus' movements, though enforced by unfavorable circumstances, are actually a fulfillment of prophecy. A portion of this Sunday's Old Testament lesson (Isa. 9:1-2) is quoted in that regard, in order to signal Jesus' foreordained ministry as God's Son.

Verse 17 implies a connection between John's imprisonment and Jesus' ministry. "From that time . . ."—that is, with the silencing of John—Jesus begins his public proclamations. The eschatological core of this lesson emerges from Jesus' exhortation, "Repent, for the kingdom of heaven has come near," a statement that describes current circumstances in terms of a future event. The designation of the kingdom as "of heaven" is also used by some writers as a means of avoiding the verbalizing of God's name. The word used for Jesus' speech is "proclaim," a word relating to the activity of a herald, one going ahead to announce important news.

Jesus' ministry expands through his calling of disciples (verses 18-22) (see parallels in Mark 1:16-20; Luke 6:12-16, and John 1:35-51). Matthew gives no explanation of the disciples' abruptness of decision to follow Jesus; either his authority was so immediately apparent, or they may have had earlier contact with him.

Jesus' assertion that his new disciples would be "fishers of people" alludes to their profession. What they will be doing has increased in significance, but this new calling parallels the old profession in several recognizable ways.

The symbolism of fishing as a missionary enterprise, however, is not original to Jesus (cf. Matt. 13:47; Luke 5:1-11; John 21:4-8). One of the most powerful uses of this symbol occurs in a portion of Ezekiel's vision of the temple (Ezek. 47:10) in which fishing figures as part of the reestablishment of God's reign. The call to follow may be compared with other Hebrew Scriptures and New Testament passages (see the call of Elisha, 1 Kings 19:19-21).

Verse 23 concludes this section in the lectionary. Jesus' tasks are threefold: to teach, to preach, and to heal. It is noteworthy that he taught in the villages' central meeting places, the synagogues of the region. This indicates that he was accepted in the areas that he visited and in which he ministered.

Matthew also use two categories of illness that Jesus cured—"disease" and "sickness"—words that seem to differ little from each other. The repetition of these two similar descriptive nouns suggest that the healings were spiritual and physical in nature: according to the Greek, they could refer to illnesses ranging from "weakness of spirit" to the soul's disfigurement through vice or depression.

Another phrase that has significance for all of Matthew's Gospel is "the people" (v. 23). It can be found fourteen times in Matthew and refers to the nation of Israel. "The people," for Matthew, have a particular link to the covenant.

HOMILETICAL REFLECTIONS

The lessons for this Sunday present several challenges related to their assigned lectionary framework, historical and social context, and familiarity.

Although the preacher will attempt to make Epiphany different from Christmas, the lectionary verse assignments for the Old Testament lesson truncate a logical rhetorical unit in the Isaian text: a messianic oracle that runs through verses 2-7. It would seem that the logic and intention of the first four verses suffer without the inclusion of the last three.

Since Year A features this text in its entirety less than a month earlier on Christmas Day, and since many do not attend worship on that day but during the evening hours of the previous night, the proclaimer may wish to preach the entire oracle during Epiphany.

Admittedly, it would be highly unusual to find a preacher who preached the Old Testament lesson on Christmas Day so, given this second appearance in the lectionary cycle, a sermon can be constructed that contrasts and compares Epiphany and Christmas interpretations of the text. That is, what does this lesson feel like now that the adult Jesus, in view of his baptism and this Sunday's Gospel, has begun his ministry as the Son of God?

This Old Testament text also deals particularly with themes of captivity and release. Any number of contemporary personal and corporate examples

THIRD SUNDAY AFTER THE EPIPHANY

of physical, spiritual, and psychological entrappment may be utilized as sermon material. The power and existence of forms of captivity continue to confront the possibilities of freedom presented by the Gospel.

What makes this text particularly poignant is the reality that liberation is often only partial rather than complete, sporadic rather than permanent. Isaiah's words witness to the eschatological hopes that persist in God's people despite historical events.

The alternative Old Testament lection, Amos 3:1-8, has a decidely different tone from the other Hebrew Scripture as well as the Gospel text. It is similiar, however, to Paul's challenges to an erring community.

Verse 7 of the Amos text raises the right of God's "servants the prophets" to speak God's intentions and "secrets."

A sermon may also be woven between a comparison of Amos and Paul's understandings of the Gospel's challenge to servanthood. The question that could be posed is, How is the call of God responded to in community? Verse 7 of the Amos text raises the right of God's "servants the prophets" to speak God's intentions and "secrets."

Paul's own view of his servitude for Jesus' sake also enables him to call a community to account under the aegis of God's eschatological reign. The confrontational harshness of Amos undoubtedly raises unavoidable issues of accountability and repentance. Paul's sarcasm in defining the problems in the Corinthian community do the same. In preaching either of these Old Testament texts, the focus on the Messiah and the call to repentance reflect and nuance the identical themes found in the epistle and stated clearly by Jesus in the Gospel.

Extrabiblical text consultation is important prior to preaching the epistle in order to gain the clearest possible sense of *context*. Particularly during the last decade, biblical research in areas related to social history, rhetoric, and feminism have raised significant issues about Paul's responses, his standing in the Corinthian faith community, his authority as an apostle with Corinth and his modes of argumentation.

A sermon created in the same epistolary form as Paul's thinking may prove interesting to a congregation as a means of amplifying his theological dialogue. Parishioners are well aware of different types of stock letters and their impact; these include "Dear John" letters and those beginning "We have not yet received your payment," or "We regret to inform you that. . . ."

Since there is no available "correspondent from Corinth," the composition and spiritual condition of the new community can only be understood through Paul's arguments. His silences and contradictions also speak clearly and should be noted by the preacher.

What makes the 1 Corinthians letter exciting are the fragmentary reflections of a growing church struggling with new ideas, willing to speak theologically, impassioned for the faith, uncertain about what form of ecclesiology best fits them. Paul's own problematic tone may be adopted, or his text may be preached as a reflection of a concerned pastor willing to engage those struggling to make sense of the power of Jesus Christ and his cross.

A sermon focusing on the issues and lives of three communities could be developed by linking with Paul's letter the two attitudes expressed in both Old Testmament lessons. What issues did each face? How did they respond?

The Gospel like the epistle, raises issues of ecclesiology and contemporary society that require a thoughtful proclamation of Jesus' ministry and the calling of the disciples. The *shape of community* is a major theme dominating the Epiphany landscape. Not only are God's people "on the road" as the committed seekers prefigured by the magi, but they are also "marching in place." That poses the questions, What do my/our ministries look like in this place and at this time? How do we feel about it? What needs changing?

The content of Jesus' ministry—teaching, preaching, and healing—may be used as one view of how faithful disciples carry out these special activities in the faith community of today. Who does them? Are any omitted or overlooked? What role do laity and leadership enact in the community as the called of the Lord?

Inescapably connected with the role of women as disciples of Jesus Christ today is a question "raised against the text." No account of women called as disciples appears in Matthew 4. This renders this historical picture problematic at its very public reading and requires the proclaimer to give careful thought to fidelity to the text *and* contemporary evidences of the Spirit's work in the church.

The preacher may also wish to contrast the calling of the disciples in this Sunday's Gospel with the account found in John's Gospel of the previous Sunday, perhaps as part of a sermon series on the dynamics of discipleship. What differing view of the call to follow Jesus do these accounts present? What specific elements of the call do they highlight, and why?

Another Epiphany theme that shows itself in all the texts is the *hiddeness of the Gospel*. Beginnings are often small, tangled in difficulties, and subject to reinterpretation. Ministry may begin out of curiosity, loyalty, allegiance, or the desire for personal gain. In all cases, the Lord of the Nations works in and through human responses of all types to bring salvation to the nations.

Fourth Sunday after the Epiphany

Lectionary	First Lesson	Psalm	Second Lesson	Gospel
Episcopal	Micah 6:1-8	Ps. 37:1-18 or 37:1-6	I Cor. 1:(18-25), 26-31	Matt. 5:1-12
Roman Catholic	Zeph. 2:3; 3:12-13	Ps. 146:6-10	I Cor. 1:26-31	Matt. 5:1-12a
Revised Common	Micah 6:1-8	Psalm 15	I Cor. 1:18-31	Matt. 5:1-12
Lutheran	Micah 6:1-8	Ps. 27:1-9	I Cor. 1:26-31	Matt. 5:1-12

FIRST LESSON: MICAH 6:1-8

Micah 6:1—7:7 features a series of recriminations against Israel. Undoubtedly, the centerpiece of Michah's reasoning is in 6:8, as it summarizes the essence of the truly righteous life before God, one manifesting justice, kindness, and humility as the ultimate expressions of the religous person (cf. Amos 5:24; Hosea 2:19-20; 6:6; Isa. 9:7; 30:15). Micah is obviously addressing those who understand the religious life as a set of cultic observances or ritual without substance.

The form of these verses is open to debate. Possibly the question-answer format bespeaks a certain type of liturgical Genre of "entrance liturgies" (see Psalms 120-134 and Isa. 33:14b-16). Or it may be understood as a controversy, a covenental lawsuit in which the plaintiff, the Lord, holds the defendant, Israel, accountable. In its current form, the controversy is not fully developed. While the history of God's dealing is explored with the people, it does not culminate in a series of accusations typical of this format. Israel is reminded, however, of the God who redeems and also of the ultimate emptiness of cultic acts done without regard for others.

The lawsuit is established in verses 1-2 by God's challenge to the people and the calling of witnesses; in fact, all creation is called to participate against Israel—"the mountains," "the hills," and even "the foundations of the earth."

Verses 3-5, review the saving acts of God in history by listing the redemption of Israel from Egypt; the blessings of leadership by men and women of God ("Moses, Aaron, and Miriam"); deliverance from evil rulers, and finally the arrival of the people in their new land (see also Numbers 22-24). The events bespeak the need for faithfulness and obedience toward God who is faithful to the people.

Verses 6-7 use hyperbole—"thousands of rams," " ten thousands of rivers of oil"—to show the extent to which cultic activity in and of itself is useless. The sarcasm culminates in the question of whether sacrificing one's firstborn child would be sufficient.

37

The entire issue of sacrifice and its place in the cultic life of Israel over the centuries is complicated (see Amos 5:21-24; Isa. 1:10-17; Isa. 40:16; Ps. 51:16-17). The reference in 6:7 possibly alludes to tragedies of human sacrifice in Israel's past, although the practice was never commanded in any way. Sources disagree.

FIRST LESSON: ZEPHANIAH 2:3; 3:12-13

Zephaniah 2:3 follows a set of harsh judgments rendered against Israel. Here the tone changes to one of invitation, with the emphasis on "Seek!" This injunction is repeated in many biblical texts (cf. Isa. 55:6-9; Amos 5:6-7). The seeking involves the Lord's command to search for righteousness and humility. The verse ends with a conditional and unnerving "perhaps" in relation to the escape from judgment.

The verses of chapter three announce that God will leave a "remnant," a people characterized by humility, lowliness, and what verse 9 refers to as a people of "pure speech." However meek and mild the remnant is, nevertheless they will not allow themselves to be intimidated: "no one shall make them afraid" (v. 13). Indeed, their "refuge in the name of the Lord" empowers them and amounts to security and a new orientation in life. (see also Ezek. 34:13-16 [reminiscent of Psalm 23] and Zech. 8:3, 16).

SECOND LESSON: I CORINTHIANS 1:18-31

This entire passage is richly rhetorical in that Paul purposefully utilizes many language strategies of his time to emphasize his key message: Christ crucified. Since there are so many of these rhetorical devices, and they play a central role in Paul's persuasive tactics, it is worth noting some of them.

Verse 18 establishes an antithesis between opposite ways of perceiving the same reality (the cross): for one group it gives life and for the others it is foolishness. Paul makes the same point in verse 19 through a "chiasmus"—making a contrast twice, only reversing the same terms. He heightens his insistence by asking three questions in verse 20, demanding the presence of an able respondent to his claims. Verses 21-24 each contain an antithesis.

Of particular importance are verses 19 and 20. Here Paul begins his great reversal of the usual definitions of wise and foolish. Paul's key terms become even more intricately developed as the reversal is explored in verse 27. For example, "foolish" could mean those spiritually or intellectually ignorant, or it could indicate those who are "foolish" enough to believe in the cross!

Most significant is the issue of the "things that are not." The God who brings something out of nothing is "the source of your life" (v. 30). This source provides wisdom, righteousness, sanctification, and redemption. There is "nothing" left apart from God. Only in God in Jesus Christ do we find "something" or "someone" of which to boast!

This passage is typical of some of Paul's greatest and most complex arguments. They are set within a culture that valued wisdom and eloquence (philosophy and rhetoric). There is much to plumb here homiletically. The homilist must be cognizant of the additional templates of Judaic wisdom traditions, gnostic influences, the rhetorical elements of the arguments, and a newly developing faith dynamic placed over the arguments.

GOSPEL: MATTHEW 5:1-12

Parishioners readily recognize this passage as "The Sermon on the Mount" or the "Beatitudes." It is also appointed for the feast day of All Saints on November 1st. These opening verses of chapter five are actually part of a longer section of Matthew, 5:1—7:27, which is understood to be the entire Sermon on the Mount.

The Gospel of Matthew can be divided into a set of five discourses of which this is the first (see also chaps. 10, 13, 18 and 24–25). Matthew may have been attempting to mirror the five books of the Pentateuch in order to show that Jesus' teaching reflects the final fulfillment of the Law.

Jesus begins by addressing his disciples alone (v. 1); his words are not meant for the crowds. Other Scriptures attest to the symbolic importance of ascending a "mountain"; such a place is considered to be the site for revelation and instruction in God's will. Matthew refers to Jesus' mountain appearances in terms of his relationship with God, instruction of his disciples, ministry activities, and as a place of meditation and prayer (cf. Matt. 4:8; 5:1; 14:23; 15:29; 17:1; 28:16). A mountain site will also be the setting of Epiphany's final Sunday, the feast of the Transfiguration. These references are noteworthy as Matthew's efforts to portray clearly Jesus as God's Son.

The "beatitudes," which extend through verse 10, are a literary form whose opposite is called the "woes," and both occur in various forms throughout the Bible (e.g., Eccles. 10:16-17). Matthew's inclusion of them may be another way in which he acknowledges Jesus as the fulfillment of the Law and the Prophets, for example, as expressed in Isaiah 61:1-3.

Verse 3 begins with Jesus' reference to the poor in spirit and their inheritance, the kingdom of heaven. Poverty does *not* refer merely to a personal attitude or material state of affairs, but to the quality of one's relationship with God: life lived mindful of the reign of God now and more fully to come. As in the other beatitudes, one should note that the verb is in the future tense and that Matthew makes use of a reversal: The poor, the have-nots, will receive everything!

What is the quality of mourning of which verse 4 speaks? Again, this verse does not laud a state of sorrow as blessed in and of itself. Instead, the reasons behind the mourning are essential. A Sorrow over the sins and failures of humanity, both personal and corporate, is the essential precursor to repentance and contrition (see Ezra 10:6; Psalm 51:4; Dan. 9:19-20; Rom. 7:24; 1 Cor. 5:2; 2 Cor. 12:21). God's response to the opening of the heart in this way is to give comfort.

Verse 5, like the two preceding it, features a word that is often misunderstood: *meek*. Meek can have many definitions, some of them insufficient. Here its sense parallels verse 3, by indicating an attitude of receptiveness toward others that springs from deeper sources of gentleness and self-control. It does not mean, however, an attitude of base servility, as is exemplified by the obsequious character of Uriah Heep, in Charles Dicken's *David Copperfield*!

"The earth" is the form of inheritance that such an attitude toward life brings. Certainly the matter of land, (e.g., the promised land) figures prominently in Judaic history and life. Yet, this phrase may well allude to the greater messianic, eschatological hopes of what is to come (cf. Psalm 37:9, 11, 29).

The most important Matthean word in verse 6 is *righteousness*. The priority placed on desiring righteousness is emphasized through the language of physical hunger and thirst. The quality of this righteousness is open to discussion. In its most encompassing sense, it can mean the desire to see righteousness worked out in personal and corporate life; in another sense it means the desire to inherit the perfection of the realized messianic kingdom (Matt. 14:20). This verse also reflects traditional themes of eschatological feasting and the Eucharist (see Jer. 31:25; Isa. 55:1; Ps. 27:1-9, which is also the Psalm for the day in the Lutheran lectionary).

Verse 7 offers the most correspondent form of reciprocity: the merciful will in turn receive mercy. While "mercy" can refer to specific acts, it is also a way of life that is open to both giving and receiving compassion, kindness, and acts of love. It can be defined as "pity," although that word usually carries overtones of condescension. Matthew refers to mercy in several passages: 6:12-15; 9:13; 12:7; 18:33-34.

Purity "pure in heart" has many meanings. It can mean a wholesome moral life, a wholehearted commitment to faith, or, deriving from these two, a public commitment to "law and order" (cf. Deut. 10:16; Ps. 24:4; Isa. 1:10-17; Ps. 51:4-17; Gen. 50:5-6; Prov. 22:11). Only the singleness and clarity of a pure heart will merit the sight of God, whose presence does not tolerate impurity of any kind (Heb. 12:14; Rev. 21:22-27).

The mention of "peacemakers" in verse 9 clearly signals the need for such persons. Their relationship to God as "children of God" reflects that of the one who has initially made our peace with God—the Son of God, Jesus Christ. (For other scriptural references to peace, see Prov. 15:1; Isa. 9:6-7; 52:7; Heb. 12:14; 1 Peter 3:11.)

The final beatitude, in verse 10, tells of those who are persecuted for righteousness' sake, whose inheritance is identical to that of the poor in spirit—the kingdom of heaven. The conclusion to the beatitude collection is somber, the reality of embattlement acknowledged. We do not know precisely how Christians were persecuted in Matthew's time, but whatever the sources of it, Jesus promises the inheritance of the kingdom for those who endure it.

Verses 11-12 are an amplification of the final beatitude. The specific form of persecution—slander—is spelled out as is the reality that the prophets have been persecuted earlier. The consequence of the life of the righteous is not, in one sense, a state of blessedness at all; the messianic kingdom has yet to come in its fullness. The faithful should not be surprised at the ensuing trauma that ushers it in.

HOMILETICAL REFLECTION

The fourth Sunday after the Epiphany stands at the chronological midpoint of the season. Because the Gospel text is so well known, it is difficult to avoid preaching on it or to overlook the influence it continues to exert in the life of the Christian community.

How should one preach these verses: as invitation? challenge? judgment? radical demand? faithful promise? grounds for crucifixion? the basis for an impassioned love affair between God and God's own people? Because Matthew's Gospel presents many materials related to the issue of "rewards and punishment," care must be taken not to preach the beatitudes from a moralistic standpoint by reducing the attributes and actions listed to merely a set of behaviors.

It may be useful to provide some historical background for listeners related to the "blessings and woes" and their function and place in the life of Israel. Additionally, one could explore the ways in which this powerful text has been scripted in various times and places in the Christian church—reassurance in one sense that this simple yet complex passage is a treasure that continues to unfold!

Various traditions may see themselves reflected in some of these understandings. The beatitudes have been considered a restatement of key

Old Testament community and spiritual values; they also may be considered an "interim ethic," a way of life between birth and the return of the Lord. In one way, they set up such an "impossible" way of life that the listener must acknowledge the true source of the faith ethic—God's grace and presence in Jesus Christ—as the way to live out the demands the beatitudes set forth. If the congregational context demands it, the preacher may wish to devote part of the sermon to a specific beatitude.

All the day's texts lend themselves to ways of answering the question, What does the holy life look like? In a time of renewed interest in the "virtues and vices," or a spiritual way of looking at life, the homilist may also wish to explore some key themes that all the lessons present in one form or another: "doing justice," "walking humbly," "showing mercy," living as the "blessed" of God.

Both the Old Testament and epistle texts offer material to supplement the preaching of the Gospel or can act as texts with the beatitudes as a key component. These lessons relate to problems that have erupted in faith communities: Some people have mistaken the form of the religious life for its content; for example the ceremonial forms of the cultic life are more important than care for human beings. Others have involved themselves in theological disputes that have split their communities and called into question the ways in which they are living out their baptismal vows and eucharistic relationships.

The reaction of the prophets and the apostle are certainly appropriate to the situation. They are pastorally concerned that the people understand the priorities of the faith life. Certain issues demand attention, and the tone of the texts' authors must reflect itself in impassioned preaching.

One possibility is to link the Beatitudes with the Micah text, which exaggerates the cultic demands only purposefully to revalue them in a different way. The Beatitudes provide the responses the prophet seeks to his questions. If it isn't "ten thousand rivers of oil" or "thousands of rams," what then *does* the Lord want?

Zephaniah uses the word *remnant* to describe God's beloved. This word will resonate with some listeners, especially the tailors and sewers. An accomplished sewer will acknowledge that a store's remnant table often provides precisely that needed piece of cloth which no other fully wrapped bolt of material can provide.

The remnant, because of its unique size, color, or shape, is valued for fulfilling the exact needs of the sewer. Often an overlooked piece of material, remnants are known to take centerstage in some sewing ventures. In fact, *only* remnants produce the beauty and warmth of quilts! A most felicitous name that some Native Americans apply to these collections of remnants is a "vision blanket"!

Paul's questions in the epistle concerning what is wise and what is foolish may be asked also in relationship to the Beatitudes. As all the texts show, outward actions and inward attitudes must correspond, in order to express what Søren Kierkegaard named again as "purity of heart to will one thing."

Fifth Sunday after the Epiphany

Lectionary	First Lesson	Psalm	Second Lesson	Gospel
Episcopal	Hab. 3:1-6, 17-19	Psalm 27 or 27:1-7	I Cor. 2:1-11	Matt. 5:13-20
Roman Catholic	Isa. 58:7-10	Ps. 112:4-9	I Cor. 2:1-5	Matt. 5:13-16
Revised Common	Isa. 58:1-9a, (9b-12)	Ps. 112:1-9, (10)	I Cor. 2:1-12, (13-16)	Matt. 5:13-20
Lutheran	Isa. 58:5-9a	Psalm 112	I Cor. 2:1-5	Matt. 5:13-20

FIRST LESSON: ISAIAH 58:5-12

This text comes from the latter part of the book called Third Isaiah. Cast in the form of a dialogue between Yahweh and the Israelites, the text reveals further the necessary contours of the godly community. One may surmise from the missing side of the argument that Isaiah is speaking against those who have defined the spiritual life in terms of cultic activity and have forgotten the intrinsic links between cult and service to one's sisters and brothers.

The major focus of the chapter can be summed up in a single question: What does it mean to fast? As with any outward action, the religious person needs to think about corresponding inner attitudes. What motivates the one who fasts? Why is fasting necessary to leading a religious life?

Verses 5-7 are a series of questions concerning fasting. Verse 5 poses three questions about the physical appearance and actions of the one fasting. This verse lyrically describes the attitude of humility by comparing a bowed head to a bulrush and mentions fasting apparel, consisting of sackcloth and ashes.

One could expect the respondent to answer "Yes!" to each of the questions and rightly so, but the verse is a set up! If the answers are yes, verse 6 signals that everything must be reoriented with a new definition that focuses the action of the one fasting within the context of community activities.

What makes the description of fasting in verse 5 so ironic, even offensive, is that cultic fasting is generally an option for the well-to-do and those who eat on a regular basis. The following verses demonstrate new transactions with regard to who feeds and to who is fed and why.

Verses 6-7 list the characteristics of the true fast, no longer a matter of chosen, physical, temporary deprivation. Instead, major Isaian themes are repeated: feeding and clothing the poor and addressing matters of injustice. Verses 8-9 discuss the effects of these actions on the one who is "fasting": spiritual enlightenment, healing, and God's response and vindication.

Verses 9c-10 restate the same ideas as verses 6-7, and verses 11-12 use both natural and architectural imagery to emphasize the spiritual well-being of those who understand the true nature of fasting. The imagery is lyrically pleasing in its description of the true ethical life before God, one that differs radically from one more set of cultic obligations. The text clearly shows that the condition of one's spiritual relationship to God is directly connected to the ways in which one actively responds to those in the community who are suffering in any way.

FIRST LESSON: HABAKKUK 3:1-6, 17-19

These verses are excerpted from the final chapter of this prophetic book and appear to be liturgical in derivation, given the psalm-like musical directions that appear in three different places. This hymnic chapter is the prophet's final faithful response to God.

The picture of God that Habakkuk draws is a God of power, a God of the land, and a God whose appearance shakes the forces of nature. Some of the imagery probably derives from pagan versions of ancient storm god images of that locale. The description of God's devastating effects upon the landscape are reminiscent of other theophanic materials (cf. Exod. 15:14-16; Judges 5:4-5; Joel 2:10).

Verses 17-19, which conclude the book and the lesson, leave the reader with the picture of a devastated land. Crops have failed, livestock is absent, and the fields lay empty of sustenance. Has the prophet ended on a profoundly sour note? Although the landscape indicates obvious evidence of God's judgment against a faithless people, the prophet nevertheless is able to reassert his faith in God.

SECOND LESSON: I CORINTHIANS 2:1-16

This Sunday's lections range from a choice of the first five verses of chapter two to a reading of the entire chapter. The former presents the conclusion of Paul's discussion of the meaning of "Christ crucified" as God's wisdom, begun in chapter one. The remainder of chapter two is a discussion of what spiritual wisdom, humanly speaking, consists of.

Paul's argument is very complex, given his philosophical and religious sources, his audiences and his purposes. In verse 4, he introduces the role of the Spirit in the wisdom of the faithful. Here he link the concepts "Spirit and power," which are found in other places as well (cf. Luke 1:35; Acts 1:8; 10:38; Rom. 15:13, 19).

FIFTH SUNDAY AFTER THE EPIPHANY

After claiming in chapter one that humans cannot speak the wisdom of God, Paul paradoxically goes on to assert in verse 6 that indeed the spiritually "mature" speak it. In verse 9, Paul quotes Isaiah 64:4 in order to buttress his argument.

Verse 12 is perhaps a truly unnerving statement. In some sense Paul seems to be certifying that through God's Spirit, we do actually know God's own mind, or at the very least, we discern the nature of God's gifts. The heightened spiritual capacities of the "mature" are further elaborated in verse 15. Having the mind of Christ—perfect wisdom, that is—the mature faithful are "subject to no one's scrutiny," or at least not from those who are "unspiritual." Paul's claim is based on the fact that this happens through one's relationship to God in Christ—who is also subject to no one's scrutiny, a fact that Paul supports with another statement from Isaiah.

GOSPEL: MATTHEW 5:13-20

This section of Matthew continues the three-chapter series of Jesus' sayings called the Sermon on the Mount. The verses readily fall into two sections: the first, verses 13-16, discusses the nature of the disciples' witness to the world; the second, verses 17-20, addresses the relationship between Jesus and the Judaic religious tradition.

In verse 13 Jesus compares the disciples' effectiveness to the flavoring and preservative power of a common element—salt. He poses a question that can have several possible answers: If the salt has lost its taste, how can it be restored? Because salt is a stable chemical compound, it is questionable whether such a thing could even happen! In other words, it can never lose its saltiness and neither can the disciples.

On the other hand, salt can mix with other substances in such a way that its strength is diluted and it becomes ineffective. The disciples may very well become ineffective. Since life itself is impossible without salt, the lives of the faithful are, by analogy, essential to the life of the gospel. The loss of faithfulness is the loss of life itself. Whatever the answer, Jesus' very question, stated in a negative form, stems from a rabbinic mode of thinking that prompts deeper pondering on the matter. Perhaps it resembles a zenlike statement!

In verses 14-16, the disciples' witness is compared to another pervasive, common reality—light. Jesus' positive affirmation of the power of light, a common religious symbol, depicts the disciples as bearers of truth, discernment, clarity, and knowledge. All of these can be symbolized by light and result in "good works" (v. 16). These are "good" only inasmuch as they reflect God and not human ability. In turn, others respond to the light of God, through these deeds, by glorifying God.

Significantly, in this verse, Matthew names the object of glorifying as "your Father in heaven." The designation of God as "Father" occurs repeatedly in Matthew as he clearly affirms that Jesus is God's Son.

The second section of these verses, verses 17-20, takes up the urgent issue of Jesus' relationship to the religious traditions of the Hebrew Scriptures. "Prophets" at the time of Jesus referred to Joshua, Judges, Samuel, Kings, Isaiah, Jeremiah, Ezekiel, and the twelve minor prophets.

In preaching other parts of Matthew's Sermon on the Mount, it will become obvious how important this section is, because it raises a cluster of issues: the relationship of the traditions; Jesus' possible abrogation, or at least diminution, of the importance of the Mosaic Law for his gospel; and the links between Law and Gospel.

What Jesus means by "fulfilling" the Law or the Prophets is open to question. It does signify his intention somehow to maintain a relationship of continuity with them. Preaching other portions of the gospel in view of this complex announcement is the only long term way to respond to it. The verses in and of themselves do not fully answer the theological questions raised in this context.

Verse 19 refers to the "commandments." Which commandments these are is not clear from the context. They could be the Ten Commandments, Jesus' preceding allusions to those commandments contained in the Law and Prophets or even his own speech inclusive of the other traditional commandments. The use of "lesser/greater" language is typical of other Synoptic sources and the gradations are applied to the ways in which others live in conformity to the gospel.

The demand to be righteous, even beyond "the scribes and Pharisees," establishes an impossible standard. The listener must refer to the entire context of the Sermon on the Mount (chaps. 5–7) and ask why perfection is required when, humanly speaking, it is impossible.

HOMILETICAL REFLECTIONS

Epiphany's major themes ring clearly through the day's lections: the images of light as indicative of salvation; the cruciform shape of community (e.g., its foundation of wisdom), and the christic imperatives stating the revelation and arrival of God's rule.

Isaiah's discussion of fasting raises some interesting possibilities for contemporary hearing, some of them seemingly contradictory, but all of them focusing on those who are starved in contrast to those who are filled (but not necessary fulfilled). The preacher must take particular care with the meaning of fasting, as it might occur for religious reasons (such as the upcoming Lenten season) or for its varied cultural connotations.

FIFTH SUNDAY AFTER THE EPIPHANY

The media has shown us over the last few years that true starvation, through war and crop failure, is very much present in many parts of the world today. Those eating T.V. dinners may simultaneously watch these tragedies on their television sets. Suffering on such a massive scale in many places is very much concretized in local parish settings in which parishioners may or may not be participating in local food pantries.

Unfortunately, members of affluent cultures utilize fasting for its outward effects in relation to cultural norms of beauty and control. The epidemic of anorexia nervosa among young people seeking beauty and athletic advantage exemplifies the norms of a culture that employs the lack of food in negative rather than positive ways.

Undoubtedly, there will be congregants for whom the notion of fasting elicits realities of suffering and family problems in this regard. Sensitive acknowledgment of this issue is called for while addressing, as did the prophets, the responsibilities we all share for one another's well-being.

As with any of God's gifts, the benefits and consequences of those gifts are understood in terms of their uses. Literal deprivation of food is not the point of the text. Instead, self-denial in service of the gospel involves personal and corporate efforts of hospitality including the care of the homeless and confronting those justice hot-spots found in any community or congregation. In fact, the very feasting and sharing of table with the hungry is, paradoxically, a sign of a true fast.

The question format of the opening verse of this text demonstrates that the religious may be often hard pressed to acknowledge their need to respond to this issue at all. Literal hunger in service of the cult may be used to avoid recognizing and accepting greater realities existing in the community.

Habakkuk's concluding hymnic praise of God also occurs in the face of deprivation. But here the prophet sees clearly that even in the midst of physical want, God's plenty is experienced in the context of a fulfilling faith relationship. The enforced fast that has come through adversity has given the prophet a new discernment about what is important: in view of Habakkuk's alarms over Israel's failings, his is indeed a faith statement of great love and trust.

Unlike the prophets in the two Old Testament lessons, Paul speaks as a religious figure to a smaller, specific community. The general issue is the same, however: Of what does the true faith life consist?

In Paul's case, his attention is drawn to theological and spiritual issues within the community. Preaching Paul's arguments on wisdom offers a substantial homiletical challenge given the difficulties of this passage. The preacher may wish to concentrate instead only on the first five verses of the chapter to conclude the previous week's focus on the cross and the crucified Christ.

Alternatively, the latter half of the text—on what makes for wisdom in the community of faith—may also be preached. The preacher will need to research and preach much background material to some extent in this latter choice, including what Paul means by "wisdom," the role of the Spirit, the problematic differentiation between the wise and the not-so-wise in the latter half of the lection, and the issue of the charismatic gifts that lie behind Paul's arguments. (Paul's differentiation here between wise and foolish is not quite the same as in the first part of his argument in chapter one.)

Continuing the emphasis on appropriate faith-life behavior in community, the selection from Matthew's Gospel focuses on Jesus' dual call to the disciples to be both faithful in their witness to the kingdom and faithful in their attention to Jesus' own claims. This dual claim is the apex of the whole text. Christians are called to show concern about their spiritual life in such a way that it actually gives cause to others to rejoice over them! Another thematic focus of the Gospel might be the relationship between the old and the new traditions: their differences and similarities; their sources of life; the challenges and joys presented by total involvement in communities that address the traditions' demands seriously.

One thematic concern explicit in the Old Testament lessons and implicit in the Gospel is that of justice, of "good works." A primary theme of the Epiphany season is the multifaceted imperative to do justice among God's people as a response to and sign of the kingdom of heaven. These eschatological motifs may be worked out through a focus on the feast/fasting motifs presented by the Old Testament Scripture, together with Jesus' injunctions to act as salt and light and the impact of such actions on others.

Sixth Sunday after the Epiphany

Lectionary	First Lesson	Psalm	Second Lesson	Gospel
Episcopal	Sir. 15:11-20	Ps. 119:1-16 or 119:6-19	I Cor. 3:1-9	Matt. 5:21-24, 27-30, 33-37
Roman Catholic	Sir. 15:15-20	Ps. 119:1-2, 4-5, 17-18, 33-34	I Cor. 2:6-10	Matt. 5:17-37 or 5:20-22, 27-28, 33-34
Revised Common	Deut. 30:15-20 or Sir. 15:15-20	Ps. 119:1-8	I Cor. 3:1-9	Matt. 5:21-37
Lutheran	Deut. 30:15-20	Ps. 119:1-6	I Cor. 2:6-13	Matt. 5:20-37

As the Epiphany season draws to a close, the texts for this Sunday heighten the emphasis on growth in faith through a deepening discernment of choices and appropriate responses to daily life. In these texts the faithful are urged to realize that self-discipline and healthy community relationships are fruits of a spirituality consistent with living in accordance with God's will and law.

Jesus' response to the heritage of the Law and Prophets provides listeners with encouragement to live beyond the obvious and to discern the true roots and causes of sin and obedience to God.

FIRST LESSON: SIRACH 15:11-20

This reading is taken from a book known by such various titles as "Ecclesiasticus," the "Wisdom of Ben Sira," or the designation "Sirach," which is a Greek spelling of the name "Sira." This passage concentrates on the difficult question of free will and choice. Given traditional interpretations of the delicate balances among free will, the perennial tragedy of sin, and God's will, care must be taken with preaching these verses. This passage is, to some extent, reflective of the alternative Old Testament lesson for this day.

Verses 11-13 affirm that God is not responsible for humanity's evil choices or the evil resulting from wrong choices. Verses 14-17 present the issue of "free choice," using the extremes of fire and water to show that the human condition demands radical choice (cf. Deut. 30:19 and Jer. 21:8).

The conclusion of the chapter, verses 18-20, recapitulates the preceding verses: God's wisdom is great; God therefore knows everything about human beings and does not "command" or "give permission" to sin. The imagery of sight—the eyes of God—is used to indicate God's knowledge of all things.

FIRST LESSON: DEUTERONOMY 30:15-20

This excerpt is taken from the final of three addresses by Moses (chaps. 29-30) and occurs in the context of a reaffirmation of God's covenant with the people of Israel. It is particularly poignant as the supposed last speech Moses will give to his people in preparing his final farewell to them.

Just as with Sirach's definition of choice, Moses, too, has placed choices before the people. This comes in the form of a reaffirmation of the original Sinai Covenant given at Horeb. Here, the Israelites are on the plains of Moab.

The legal formulization and liturgical context of this passage differs from the school situation of Sirach. The hortatory wording of the text, which continues to the end of the chapter, fits that part of a covenantal renewal ceremony; first, a choice is presented (vv. 15-18), which is basically the choice between God and service to idols; then witnesses are asked to attest to the occasion (v. 19a), and finally, there is a call to decision (vv. 19b-20). A decision for God will result in "life" (a way of living) and possession of the land (see Exod. 19:3-9 and Josh. 24:15-24).

The formality of the structure, however, should not divert attention from the fact that this is more than a legal/religious juridical pronouncement; it is the final sermon of Moses to his people. It is as though Moses is responding to the question, "If I had only one thing to say, it would be. . . ."

SECOND LESSON: I CORINTHIANS 3:1-9

The opening of this chapter refers back to Paul's discussion in chapter one about dissension among the Corinthians over leadership in the community. He presents the choices he made on behalf of the Corinthians and the choices they must make in order to do God's will. Paul uses four different images to emphasize three points: why he has behaved towards them the way he has; what role Christ's missionaries play in their community; and how God perceives the Corinthian community.

In verses 1-3 Paul utilizes maternal imagery to show the Corinthians that faith insights are nurtured by appropriate actions in community (not "jealousy and quarreling"). Like a mother who must decide when a child is ready for certain foods ("infants in Christ"), so Paul has had to make the same spiritual choice—"I fed you with milk, not solid food." Thus the Corinthians should not mistake simple for simplistic teachings or want more than they can spiritually tolerate (see also Heb. 5:12-14 and 1 Peter 2:2).

In verses 4-8 Paul utilizes agricultural imagery to show that he and other missionaries to the Corinthians are like farmers who only tend what God has already established. Consequently, Paul also places the responsibility of spiritual growth in God's hand rather than his own - "only God gives the growth." That is, Paul's actions are instrumental but not originally causal.

Paul expands the imagery somewhat in verse 9 by identifying the Corinthians not as God's fellow workers but as God's field, subject to whatever a farmer God wishes to do with them! Verse 9 concludes with another image that Paul will further develop: the Corinthian's are "God's building."

While these verses provide a justification of Paul's missionary methods among the Corinthians, Paul makes it clear to them that he is not ultimately responsible for the method, the means, or the outcome. All of this lies with God.

For 1 Corinthians 2:6-13, see the Fifth Sunday after Epiphany.

GOSPEL: MATTHEW 5:21-37

These verses are the final readings from the Sermon on the Mount for the season of Epiphany. They can be divided into three sections: verses 21-26, enmity and reconciliation with sisters and brothers in the community; verses 27-32, lust, divorce, and adultery; and verses 33-37, the use of language.

The rhythm of these verses comes from the repetition of "You have heard it said. . . . But I say to you. . . ." This formula signals that homiletical decisions must be made about how to preach Jesus' relationship to the Mosaic Law. Are his statements, as a whole or individually, abrogations of the Mosaic law to some extent? Or are they intensifications? Or perhaps contradictions?

The "judgment" referred to in vv. 21-26 may be historical as well as eschatological, since communities had local courts for the settlement of disputes as dictated by the deuteronomic code (see Deut. 16:18). Jesus identifies a basic attitude of anger as a preliminary condition to murder. Deeds are only the outward manifestation of attitudes. Verses 23-24 offer concrete ways in which to defuse the anger that could potentially lead to murder.

Memory plays a vital role in the community in terms of the reconciliation Jesus asks: "If you remember that your brother or sister has something against you. . . ." Interestingly, this remark does not specify that the one remembering was the cause of the problem or that there even is a legitimate problem! In other words, if your sister or brother *perceives*, or "has an attitude," that they have something against you, this should prompt reconciliation. The gift of reconciliation must precede any gifts to God and be offered with the knowledge that anger is a sin that radically distorts and confuses the issues.

This spiritual bookkeeping is balanced against the potential for an escalating dispute that then will result in the necessity to pay "the last penny," a situation in which true injustice might exist since the situation may or may not warrant such a demand (v. 26).

Verses 27-32 take up the issue of divorce, an action that can have its roots in the profoundly dehumanizing effects of lust (see Deut. 5:21 and Exod. 20:17). Jesus utilizes hyperbole in vv. 29-30 in order to dramatize the effects and potential outcomes of inappropriate and unchecked feelings.

Since the wording of this crucial text varies in other injunctions against divorce, it is necessary to compare wordings. Modern-day listeners would easily note the absence in some sources of similar accounts of women's part in activities related to lust, marriage, remarriage, and divorce (see Mark 10:11-12; Luke 16:18; Rom. 7:2-3; 1 Cor. 7:10-11).

The final section, verses 33-37, concerns speech and the reverencing of God's name. While this is based in the Ten Commandments, the codes regarding speech extended into all areas of life (see Lev. 19:12; Num. 30:2, Deut. 23:21; Matt. 23:16-22; James 5:12).

HOMILETICAL REFLECTIONS

All of the lessons set out the necessity of choosing between a lifestyle that reflects God and one that espouses the idols of contemporary life. Each of the texts names the proximate communities of daily life—among fellow worshipers, acquaintances, between husband and wife, spiritual leaders, coworkers—as the locale where such choices must be made. These choices are not depicted in radical standoffs—believers against pagans—but rather in the context of everyday life.

Mention is also made, explicitly and implicitly, of some of the preexisting agreements or covenants that govern such relationships: the covenant between God and the Israelites; between people and their forms of governance, such as the "council" or the "Sanhedrin"; between God and God's servants; between individuals, such as a marriage relationship. Since such agreements have to do with the realities of witness, agreement, and promise, the preacher may wish to explore on what promises/vows/agreements Christians base their choices of faithful living.

Both of the Old Testament lessons concentrate on the relationship between human choice and God's command to be perfect. One author speaks as a teacher, the second, Moses, as a pastor saying a final farewell. Just

SIXTH SUNDAY AFTER THE EPIPHANY

as Jesus will speak "for the final time" in the concluding text of next's Sunday's transfiguration, so Moses speaks about what is most vital to maintain life in his last days with the Israelites. What are the characteristics of a "last will and testament"?

The second lesson readily acknowledges that the Christian life is a matter of education, degree, and the accumulation of insight over time. "Milk" and "meat" Christians simultaneously exist in all congregations, and neither depends on either age or education! The preacher may wish to use the text's maternal imagery to explore why Paul might have chosen these titles for the group at Corinth. How do they apply today and with what criteria? The "milk" appellation is not necessarily a negative one.

How do the vows/covenants/agreements we make as Christians contribute to our growth in the faith? How do we regard others who are at different levels of faith maturity? Who decides? How does the community forgive, educate, support, and encourage Christians at all levels of interaction with their God and their communities? What of those who resist growth and persist in troublemaking and dissension in the community?

Paul's words also raise the interesting issue of the relationship between people and pastor, leadership and congregation. Paul uses the word *servants* having a "common purpose." This is asserting a delicate balance between Paul as spiritual parent and Paul as a servant! It also assumes that servants have common purposes with their superiors.

The context of a given congregation's life may make this a useful passage if ministry ideas and relationships are in flux or in question. Paul certainly offers a model, with its own internal contradictions, of one who is upset and challenging, yet also lovingly concerned that the "common purpose," the establishment of Christ's reign, may be accomplished. Common purpose or cross purposes?

The Gospel text for this Sunday is, in a word, "difficult." It is so because Jesus knew that his listeners found the words troublesome, and inevitably the day's lection on divorce demands homiletical center stage and will also prompt the same response!

It is probably irresponsible not to acknowledge and preach the Gospel words for this Sunday. Parishioners are sensitive to any homiletical evasion of the topic of divorce, despite its difficulties. A humorous but significant symbol of such an unconscious congregational response occurred in one congregation in which the guest preacher noted out loud to the parish, just prior to her sermon, that after the "Hymn of the Day," the term "Sermon" was omitted in the program and the service continued, typographically speaking, without it!

Not only will the divorced, the separated, the single, and those in difficult relationships hear a sermon on divorce, but so will the children and relatives of those touched by it. The entire community may profit from hearing an open acknowledgment of this issue from the pulpit.

Preaching on such a text could entail several possibilities. The history of the divorce codes in Judaic law and contemporary thinking can be developed. As Jesus makes clear, the issue of *attitudes* is the primary factor that prefigures the reality of divorce. According to Jesus, lust is, actually *"more* than meets the eye." It is dehumanization for the purposes of abuse of the other, a possibility that can be exercised by male or female.

How do the passages specify the issue of the role of women in divorce? Do they? What were Jesus' intentions about the status and responsibilities of women in the matter of divorce?

It could be useful to preach the call for reconciliation in this passage by connecting it with the words that follow on divorce. What roles does reconciliation have between a brother and sister in the faith (e.g., a married couple)? Who initiates it? What attitudes lead to standoffs? When is reconciliation no longer a possibility? How do the unreconciled affect a community's worship? Most importantly, whatever the marriage vows, how do God's promises of presence, support, forgiveness, and ultimate faithfulness figure in matters of divorce?

Whether connected with a sermon on divorce or not, the issue of reconciliation is one that looms large in both the epistle and Gospel texts. The Matthean passage is often related directly to a eucharistic community's "table manners" through the ritual of the Exchange or Kiss of Peace.

This liturgical ritual may be acknowledged as an example of "remembering" and hoping for peace in relationships of all kinds. It is truly both a present and an eschatological act in which individuals and communities are invited to participate as an expression of their gratitude for God's peace among them.

These lessons draw to a conclusion the Epiphany season's major themes dealing with what constitutes a godly life personally and corporately, which quarrels and issues may upset or distort, what choices are called for, what responsibilities demanded. Together these themes point toward the Lenten season in which a more concentrated reenactment will occur in the Passion of Jesus—exemplar and savior of God's community; Light and Life to all.

The Transfiguration of Our Lord
Last Sunday after the Epiphany

Lectionary	First Lesson	Psalm	Second Lesson	Gospel
Episcopal	Exod. 24:12, (13-14), 15-18	Psalm 99	Phil. 3:7-14	Matt. 17:1-9
Roman Catholic	Dan. 7:9-10, 13-14	Ps. 97:1-2, 5-6, 9	2 Pet. 1:16-19	Matt. 17:1-9
Revised Common	Exod. 24:12-18	Psalm 2 or 99	2 Pet. 1:16-21	Matt. 17:1-9
Lutheran	Exod. 24:12, 15-18	Ps. 2:6-13	2 Pet. 1:16-19, (20-21)	Matt. 17:1-9

This Sunday is not only the last Sunday in Epiphany—it also acts as a mirror of the feast of the Epiphany and a recapitulation of the season's major themes. Like the Epiphany, the Transfiguration offers humanity, in its entirety, a new vision of itself and God. It is also a vision that has not drawn to its final conclusion.

The texts for this day emphasize the role of God's laws, humanity's accountability and calling in the context of faith communities, and the centrality of Jesus Christ as the fulfillment of all that has gone before. All of this is set in the encompassing reality of "the glory of the Lord," a recurring image that includes hope, redemption, new directions, discernment, and enlightenment.

FIRST LESSON: EXODUS 24:12-18

These verses feature God's gift of "the law and the commandments" to the people of Israel (cf. Exod. 32:15; 34:28; Deut. 9:9-15 for other versions). This section introduces the materials of chaps. 25–31 in which God gives Moses the prescriptions for the people's cultic life. This section concludes with Exodus 31:18: "When God finished speaking with Moses on Mount Sinai, he gave him the two tablets of the covenant, tablets of stone, written with the finger of God."

As in the preceding verses of this chapter (vv. 9-11) in which God feasts with Moses and the elders of Israel, these verses also contain a revelation of God, a theophany, in which God's glory is covered by a cloud and is also "like a devouring fire (v. 17). This second theophany (possibly another strand of the tradition?), however, is restricted to Moses and results in the giving of God's commandments to the people.

Verse 12 is significant for it states that the purpose of the Law is for the peoples' "instruction." Moses approaches God in two stages to receive these laws: first he goes up on the mountain (v. 15) and on the seventh day he enters the cloud and stays there for forty days and nights (cf. Deut. 10:1-5 for what might be an earlier tradition of the giving of the Law).

FIRST LESSON: DANIEL 7:9-10; 13-14

Like the Exodus text, this passage emphasizes the role of God's judgment and law. The verses come from the only Old Testament apocalyptic book. "Daniel" is probably a pseudonym for a Jewish author who is attempting to understand Jewish history in an eschatological fashion. In order to give credence to writings, names of notable individuals were borrowed from other sources, and "Daniel" may be the person referred to in Ezek. 14:14 and 28:3. Although contemporary opinion would deem this to be plagiarism, the acceptability of such pseudonyms in ancient times witnesses to the common hopes of an entire people for salvation. Like the proclaimer's exegetical mysteries concerning the identity of the Isaian "servant," the point is not *who* is the author, but the content and purpose of the message.

Chapter seven contains one of Daniel's four dream-visions along with its interpretation. The overall intention of the book, and this entire chapter, is to offer Jews the hope of God's final vindication, despite the metaphoric lurid violence of the vision. Verses 11-12 are omitted from the lection because they refer to such historic actualities as the impending destruction of the Greek empire and might thus diminish the vision's impact.

Verses 9-10 present a revelation of God, "the Ancient One." While this reinforces the usual stereotypic view of "old man God on a throne," the visionary vividness that follows rearranges the concept sufficiently! The images describing God are based on light, fire, and movement: "his clothing was as white as snow"; the throne's wheels (it apparently was in motion!) "were burning fire"; fire "flowed out from his presence"; and those who serve are both serving him and standing in attendance. The setting is juridical, judgment will be rendered based on what is found "in the books [which] were opened."

Verses 13-14 present a "human being" who is ushered into the Ancient One's presence. The setting and intent of this passage is similar to Isaiah 42 in which the servant is introduced at court. Jurisdiction is handed over to the "human being" and it is eternal and all-inclusive, embracing "all peoples, nations, and languages." The kingship will also be permanent; it "shall never be destroyed."

There are several possible identifications of the "human being." Based on other references in Daniel, it could be the Jews' patron angel, Michael (10:13, 21; 12:1). It may be the archetypal faithful Jew whom God will save and bless. Later traditions have generally understood the figure in

THE TRANSFIGURATION OF OUR LORD

messianic terms. The layering of the traditions witnesses to the Epiphany theme of God's revelations—often subtle, gradual, perhaps even unexpected.

SECOND LESSON: PHILIPPIANS 3:7-14

Paul sets up a radical disregard for all that he might have possessed prior to knowing Christ, in view of the salvation he has now received and experienced through Jesus Christ. This passage is openly autobiographical in its intent to describe Paul's own spiritual journey and thereby encourage others in theirs.

Verse 7 speaks of "gains" that Paul formerly had. These might possibly have been all those spiritual and societal assets he had as a highly educated and powerful Jew of his time. Other assertions about "being nothing" elsewhere could very well stem from his loss of social and religious status, as well as from his perceived state before God.

Paul emphasizes just how worthless these things have become by dismissing them as "refuse" (v. 8), a word not translated to its full extent but in some sources, at least, rendered as "dung." Homiletical choice and discretion may decide how much emphasis to give this translation. Paul finds he cannot be emphatic enough in describing the contrast between his former way of life and his new life in Christ. The righteousness of God that Paul now possesses comes to him as God's gift in Jesus, unlike his former efforts to be godly through the law.

Verses 10-11 list three realities that Paul wishes to share with Christ: "the power of his resurrection"; "sharing of his suffering" (note: sharing—not repeating them!); and "becoming like him in his death." These verses define comprehensively the list of the activities that comprise the sanctified life.

Paul uses an athletic metaphor to describe the arduous yet pleasing endeavor of the sanctified life in Christ. Just as a runner seeks the goal without wasting time looking behind, so Paul fastens on Jesus Christ as "the prize of the heavenly call of God," one who is both goal and prize simultaneously! The passage sets an eschatological tone for the reading of the Gospel.

SECOND LESSON: 2 PETER 1:16-21

Traditionally, this biblical book purports to have been authored by Peter, another apostle of Jesus Christ. Although this is probably not the case, Peter's witness of the transfiguration is a crucial part of actual or perceived historical testimony in the Christian tradition.

Verse 16 establishes that the transfiguration was an historical event and that Peter witnessed "his majesty." This visual sign of God was further emphasized through an auditory sign, as through "the Majestic Glory" that verbally attributed God's sonship to Jesus (v. 17).

Additionally, the prophets witness to three things: Jesus, his glory, and his return. Peter specifically links the transfiguration with Jesus' return. In a different fashion, Matthew directs the reader's attention to Jesus' upcoming passion and death.

Verse 19 offers the motif of light in three ways "until the day dawns," "as to a lamp shining in a dark place," and "the morning star rises in your hearts." In order to buttress the personal witness of verses 16-18, the writer adds that they are not idiosyncratic, "a matter of one's own interpretation," but, as in verse 21, they speak through human agency "by the Holy Spirit [who] spoke by God." In other words, Peter could not say these truthful words unless God's Spirit was inspiring him to do so.

GOSPEL: MATTHEW 17:1-9

This theophany has parallels in the other Synoptic Gospels (Mark 9:2-8; Luke 9:28-36; and New Testament texts such as Acts 9:1-19; Rev. 1:10ff.). As is typical of other biblical references to places of revelation, verse 1 notes that Jesus took three of his disciples with him "up a high mountain." What exactly happened during this event we call the transfiguration is not clearly known since the Gospel writer uses a simile to describe how Jesus looked: "His face shone like the sun" (v. 2; see Exod. 34:29).

His clothes also became "dazzling white," a scriptural symbol for the garments of divine beings. The book of Revelation notes over sixteen occurrences of such divine glory. The verb "transfigured" has a recognizable English-language meaning, "he was metamorphosed." What is significant about this verse is that Jesus himself changes appearance. In contrast to his baptismal day, when the focus is on the voice from heaven, Jesus himself assumes the garments and appearance of glory here.

Verse 3 describes the simultaneous appearance of both Israel's chief giver of the Law, Moses, and a prophet, Elijah, appearing with Jesus. Both men had also received instructions from God on a mountaintop and witnessed God's glory (cf. Exod. 31:18 and 1 Kings 19:11). They are talking with Jesus and Peter joins the conversation in verse 4, remarking that it is good for him and his two companions to be there. (Peter's mention of booth building could refer to the feast of the Tabernacles; see Lev. 23:42-43.)

Peter is interrupted by God in Verse 5! As only Matthew notes, the "bright" cloud's voice must command Peter's silence and attention. Not

THE TRANSFIGURATION OF OUR LORD

only does the godly voice of Jesus' baptism speak, but it is followed by the further injunction to "listen to him!" These words, as Matthew reports them, are found also in the lesson from the Baptism of Our Lord from the First Sunday after the Epiphany (Isa. 42:1) and in the royal oracle of Psalm 2:7.

The booth building must be put on indefinite hold, because God shows Peter that Jesus, and not Moses and Elijah, should be the focus of Peter's attention. Peter's response here should be read within the context of his own earlier affirmation of Jesus as the Messiah (Matt. 16:16). God's command to the disciples is significant, even urgent, since this event marks the beginning of Jesus' instruction and activities that will lead to his death (see Deut. 18:15-18; Acts 3:22-23; 7:37).

Verses 6-8 conclude the theophany. The disciples are so fearful they fall to the ground and are only revived by Jesus' physical touch and verbal assurance. He does not offer them an explanation of what has just happened. Still overwhelmed, the disciples see "no one except Jesus himself alone."

HOMILETICAL REFLECTIONS

The concluding verse of the Gospel text for this day perhaps best sums up the reality of the faith journey. We, like the disciples, have had some intimations of glory, but also like the disciples we live during the interim time with "no one except Jesus himself alone." It is the sum total of the message of Epiphany.

The homilist's peculiar tasks on this day are challenging. The texts and themes summarize the Epiphany season and vividly remind the listeners that it is a time of paradoxes and spiritual tensions.

Above all, it is essential to enjoy and preach the power and the glory without attempting rational explanations about the *how* of this momentous occasion. The transfiguration can be understood in many ways: an historical event defying description; a post-resurrection narrative that found its way into the Gospel; an initiation story or a mythopoetic way of describing the divine glory and sonship of Jesus.

The entire Epiphany season is marked by mountaintop experiences and witnesses of which this day is the culmination: "Take it from me—we were there!" Whatever hermeneutical choices the proclaimer makes concerning this event, as with the call to the disciples, *God* has set the stage for the biggest fishing story in all of human history!

Three of the day's texts are theophanies and the rest are reflections on them. The crown of these is Matthew's account of Jesus' transfiguration. It is important to reflect, however, on *why* the event happened and why Matthew and the other Gospel writers include it in their accounts of Jesus' life. This festival day is the high point of a season of profound metamorphosis on the part of Jesus, the disciples, and the nations. God's voice at Horeb and Moab, the same voice as at Jesus' baptism and finally at the transfiguration, will soon be the eloquent speech of the cross.

Another possible homiletical approach is to examine the reality of *change*, the change people experience when affected by significant events. This theme is obviously prompted by the metamorphosis that Jesus undergoes on the mountaintop, but there is more to it.

What does it mean for him—and for us—to change? People comment often on the fact that others change: "She is a changed person"; or "He hasn't been the same since. . . ." One of the more fascinating reflections on human change is the one rendered in Franz Kafka's story "The Metamorphosis." He describes the bizarre and poignant spiritual experiences of a human who is changing into a big insect! While this is a fictional rendering of the reality of change taken to an extreme, it dramatizes the boundaries and possibilities of human change.

Appropriate responses to inexplicable changes do not lie in explaining the "how" of mystical events but the way such changes affect people. The entire Epiphany season witnesses to the personal and corporate changes that Jesus' arrival caused. Perspectives changed. For example, the prophets began to articulate the "servant's" mission to *all* nations, not just Israel. In the middle of destruction, they saw for the people of Israel God's impending blessings.

Status changes occur for those touched by God. The imprisoned are set free, the committed, such as Paul, are imprisoned. The land lies absolutely desolate but the prophet sings a song of hope. The worldly wise learn another kind of wisdom and the foolish find wisdom in the cross and, like the sages, are surprised to find that they are taking another way home. "Just Jesus" is revealed as God's beloved Son.

Changes might occur in those who exchange cultic observance for justice in relationships. Truly becoming a "change agent" is the result of going through the transformation effected by the salvation of Jesus Christ and for that to affect the lives of others.

The texts and the witnesses also speak of the major thread in Epiphany's tapestry of God's *faithfulness*. The covenant was established and renewed. Witnesses were called to testify to it over the centuries. It was fulfilled in Jesus' birth to which the wisest of the sages traveled in order to worship. It was reiterated again at Jesus' baptism and finally at his transfiguration.

Clearly, however, the eschatalogical question surrounds this day: What next? Transfiguration is to be understood not as closure but as revelation; not as conclusive but as preliminary. The invitation to the mountaintop is followed by the need to descend from it and be about the things of God.

Also over this day hangs a question: Who is this Jesus? While the voice from the cloud twice affirms who it is, while the major figures of the tradition affirm his identity in prophetic speech and writing, and the post-resurrection confessions of the apostles name him, the disciples on the mountainside are caught between what they saw and "just Jesus."

They are between past and present in precisely the same way that Jesus' disciples are today. And their responses and actions are the same as ours today: fear, questioning, commitment, struggle, reconciliation, joy.

Who is Jesus? The question may be asked in the mythopoetic terms of one of the lyrical lover's questions in the Song of Songs:

> Who is this that looks forth like the dawn,
> fair as the moon, bright as the sun,
> terrible as an army with banners? (6:10)